THE INFAMOUS THEATERS OF VIRGINIA CITY, NEVADA

THE INFAMOUS THEATERS OF VIRGINIA CITY, NEVADA

CAROLYN GRATTAN EICHIN

Published by The History Press,
An imprint of Arcadia Publishing
Charleston, SC
www.historypress.com

Piper's Opera House. *Christof D. Eichin, photographer.*

First published 2025

Manufactured in the United States

ISBN 9781467159746

Library of Congress Control Number: 2025934731

Notice: The information in this book is true and complete to the best of our knowledge. It is offered without guarantee on the part of the author or The History Press. The author and The History Press disclaim all liability in connection with the use of this book.

For Joe, Heather and Sarah.

CONTENTS

PREFACE

This book is dedicated to the fine theater actors and actresses who have unfortunately passed into oblivion with our changing times. Performing in front of a live audience came with numerous challenges, especially in the booming Virginia City of the 1800s. We can never fully recover the excitement of the time when thousands called the mining town home. At over six thousand feet in elevation, one can imagine a huffing and puffing stage personality peering out over an audience of young rascals in the parquette, seasoned middle-class respectability in the dress circle seats, a gallery of working stiffs and any number of fallen women occupying the boxes on the theater's exterior walls. Liquor flowed freely; the gallery gods corrected an actor's missed lines, especially in Shakespearean plays; and all manner of hooting, hollering, foot stomping, hand clapping, whistling, singing along to the music, cigar smoking, dogs barking and free-wheeling adventuresome behaviors were observed. How could a performer even attempt to make everyone happy?

Virginia City's theaters had to be seen to be believed. Here, we can only attempt to bring a marvel of that time to fruition.

ACKNOWLEDGEMENTS

Writing a book is a joint effort—that is, there are so many people who have provided help and inspiration that it is impossible to fairly credit everyone. But to all, thank you.

I especially need to thank my husband, Chris, for his expertise with the pictures and graphics, proofreading, suggestions, good humor and understanding.

Special thanks go out to Laurie Krill for her enthusiasm, encouragement and care for many details along the way. Thanks also to all of the other kind folks at The History Press.

My deep thanks and gratitude go out to all the many librarians who helped provide sources, photographs, encouragement and general good wishes. Special thanks to the wonderful folks at University of Nevada, Reno's Special Collections, especially Anna Knapp, for her help with photographs. Thanks also to the Nevada Historical Society, Nora Stefu of the Fourth Ward School Museum, Sacramento History Center, California Historical Society and the Bancroft Library.

INTRODUCTION

[In 1876 Virginia City,] *every activity has to do with the mining, transportation, or reduction of silver ore, or the melting and assaying of silver bullion.*
—*John Powell, in* Nevada, The Land of Silver

Virginia City lies in extreme western Nevada, nestled on the eastern slopes of the Virginia Range in the shadow of Mount Davidson (Sun Mountain to the local Paiute Natives). Virginia City sprang up after the discovery of the Comstock Lode of silver ore in June 1859. Miners in neighboring Gold Hill kept throwing out the soft blue clay—silver in its natural form—that clogged the riffles on gold rush–style gold panning equipment. Placer miners would exploit the shimmering hillock in Gold Hill for three years before realizing it was an extension of a lode—a mining term indicating a large geologic deposit of ore—and that silver ore would prove more plentiful and profitable than gold. Little did they know that these wealthy precious metals would manifest as the world's greatest ore deposit and be discovered slightly north of them when a cast of wonderful characters stumbled on an outcropping soon labeled after curmudgeon Henry P.T. Comstock. Hard rock mining replaced placer mining attempts, and as the mines developed, the area's population grew.

The Comstock Lode became the richest ore body at that time. Nevada eventually became the silver state based on this discovery, and people flooded into what is now Virginia City determined to find jobs, establish

businesses, make money and enjoy life. Virginia City, the town that matured directly on top of the underground riches, became the largest city in Nevada during the 1800s.

The development of each town in the American West appears to go through stages. The earliest years drew single young men to job opportunities. Frequently, observers found similarities between Virginia City's early development and the Gold Rush years of early California. Over time, more women and families moved in, and conditions changed. Each town faced this change to a more family-oriented environment at a different time, and many of these changes can be observed by examining the transitions in the theater histories of these towns. As the demographics of a town's population changed, the theater changed in response.

Entertainment followed, in general ways, the prosperity of the mines under Virginia City's feet. More money was produced by the Comstock Lode than the entire California Gold Rush a decade before. The *Gold Hill Daily News* estimated that a stunning \$85 million (\$1.8 billion today) had been extracted from the state's mines by 1867. That estimate preceded the development of dynamite and the succeeding boom years. By 1876, Nevada

Virginia City in the 1870s, as captured by Black artist Grafton T. Brown. Mount Davidson can be seen in the background. *Special Collections Photographs, UNRS-P1373-1.tif Collection_4958; Special Collections and University Archive collection department, University of Nevada, Reno.*

had produced over half of all the precious metals in the United States; over $400 million of the coinage of the day came from Virginia City's mines. The wealth supported the Northern cause during the Civil War and flooded the world monetary markets, compelling significant economic change. Silver, considered the monetary equal of gold at the time of the Comstock Lode's discovery, assayed out at twice the value of the gold in Comstock ore; both metals occurred together geologically. Soon, the Comstock boasted some of the deepest mines in the world.

According to early mercantile directories, Virginia City blossomed as the elegant interior partner of San Francisco, which functioned as the business and population base of the region. San Francisco on the coast, and Virginia City inland, became a mantra of the mid-1860s. Dominated by San Francisco moneyed interests, Virginia City echoed San Francisco's sophistication with fine restaurants, fashion, theater and cosmopolitan charm. Mine owners who made a killing in the mines spent their wealth in San Francisco, where a stock market existed solely for the exploitation of Comstock mining. The sleepy port of 1860s San Francisco became revitalized by the Comstock Lode's discovery. San Francisco developed and grew as a cultural and financial center prospering from Virginia City's wealth. Over time, the wealth from the mines came to be consolidated in the hands of a few mine owners. A group called the "Irish Big Four" significantly influenced the industrialization of the town in support of their mining interests.

Theater history is a branch of social history—that is, the history of the people of a region as viewed through a lens of their lived experiences. Studying Virginia City's theater history provides information about settlement in the American West and brings insight into the mindset of the West's inhabitants. A businessman who saw the theater as a business, similar to others, brought a singular perspective to theater management and its subsequent outcomes. While that theater owner was white, he struggled with daily life shaped through the immigrant experience—as did the vast majority of his audience. These mindsets from other countries affected the theater in Virginia City. The popularity of the theater, realized in overflowing audiences, had the potential to be more influential than the era's lectures, books, press and pulpit.

Theater of the 1800s was dynamic. A three-act melodrama had performers out before the drop curtain, entertaining with songs and dances while the stage was being reset for the next act. No show could be considered complete without ballads and comicalities between acts or following a play, and all performers were expected to appear in an afterpiece. An afterpiece of a one-act skit often broached a comic topic and appeared after most plays other than Shakespeare's, which could run for three hours.

A majority of people who lived in the towns above the Comstock Lode—Virginia City and Gold Hill—were miners. In 1860, 30 percent of the residents were foreign-born. They came from all over the world, but people from Ireland predominated. They left Ireland to escape a famine and make better lives for themselves in America, settling in cities where they could find work; often jobs others disliked. Work in the mines was dangerous—ceilings could crash down in mining tunnels that were poorly supported, and fires could start from candles that were burned for light, or from machinery. The air in the mines could be stale or filled with noxious gases, even though blowers were used to bring in fresh air. The people who worked in mining wanted to forget their fears and enjoy their time away from the mines. In the mid-1800s, there were no televisions, movies, radios, cellphones or social media for entertainment. The only entertainment came from live performances by real people.

The earliest theater in Virginia City thrived high up on the mountainside on Howard Street. Small variety theaters, which primarily showed minstrelsy, soon followed on C Street, a main route. In 1863, a large theater of the type found in New York City and San Francisco was built on D Street, one street below C Street. Tom Maguire sold this theater to John Piper in 1867. The theater's name changed to Piper's Opera House, and it became known as the most important theater in Nevada and ranked Virginia City as second only to San Francisco in theatrical importance during its best years of operation. Piper's strategics included establishing relationships with San Francisco theaters in order to bring talent to the mining town, buying out his competition, catering to his audience's interests and exercising an ability to change as Virginia City's audiences demanded theatricalities that honored the changing cultural landscape. He rebuilt his theater buildings twice after devastating fires. His last theater still stands.

1

THE EARLY DAYS

MINSTRELSY, MUSIC AND MISCHIEF

What a strange theater this is. I look out the back window and see the desert.
—so mused Artemus Ward prior to a speaking engagement at the theater Tom Maguire established on D Street in 1863

Virginia City boomed in response to mining discoveries as people rushed to the area. The town's population totaled about seven thousand by 1863 and boomed to estimates of twenty-five thousand by the mid-1870s, giving the Virginia City area more than half of all of Nevada's population. In 1870, predominantly men were in residence, with women making up only 30 percent of the population. Not surprisingly, shows that appealed to young, single men dominated the theatricalities offered.

The *Territorial Enterprise* newspaper from September 1, 1860, reported that a "pioneer theatre" of respectable dimensions and appearance had been completed; later dubbed the "Howard Street Theatre" due to its location. The first documented theater performance in Virginia City was held there on September 29, 1860, conducted by both male and female visiting amateur actors from Utah's Camp Floyd. This first performance included a two-act play titled *Toodles,* with *The Swiss Swains*, a short comedy operetta. By November, professional entertainers from San Francisco had played the little theater.

In February 1861, a melodeon opened on C Street, offering *The Last Chance in Virginia City or the Speculator and His Jackass* for folks who liked a shot of liquor served by pretty waiter girls with their farces. Melodeons were small variety theaters of the time, and they were frequently attached to saloons. They specialized in salacious jokes, risqué costuming and coarse ribaldry. The term came from the frequently used melodeon instrument, a portable reed organ similar to but smaller and easier to move than a piano. Melodeons could easily be transported in a box under the back seat of a Concord mud wagon and then taken into saloons to play simple music. Musicians worked the bellows with their feet. The melodeon became a symbol of the pleasures offered in saloons, and the name stuck to the businesses themselves.

These unpretentious saloon-theaters offered variety entertainment—mostly minstrelsy—based on music, dancing and comedy skits performed by young men and women and often filled with inuendo and sexual references. Small stages were secondary to the sale of liquor and the availability of women. Melodeons were the forerunners of vaudeville and twentieth-century burlesque houses. Frequently, the waiter girls—always called "pretty"—took turns on stage presenting their favorite songs or dance routines, which could advertise the woman's charms if she chose to exchange sexual favors for money in addition to her waitress duties. Comedy skits usually had broad physical slapstick comedy; people slipped and fell in humorous ways onstage or created mock controversy with playful fighting, improvisational jokes and comedy based on current happenings and local gossip. The comedy skit of *Never Send Your Wife to Carson* played to Virginia City crowds who laughed uproariously. In the play, the befuddled wife returns from Carson City to find her husband in bed with another woman. It became entertainment for lonely men, as ideas of respectability kept most women at home.

A third Virginia City melodeon theater titled Topliffe's opened on July 4, 1862, on C Street, the main north–south corridor through the city. Later in 1862, Topliffe's reverted to a dance hall with imported "German girls" in slow times. The *Territorial Enterprise* recalled Topliffe's as a "palatial chebang," a term combining *she* and *bang* that emphasized the sexual nature of the theatricalities there—women in revealing clothes—and the fact that the melodeon functioned as a place to meet up with members of the opposite sex. Nearby Gold Hill also had a small theater by 1862, and it generally played variety shows—including minstrel music, dancing women and short skits—light frivolous performances designed to bring a smile to the faces of the tired miners, many of them immigrants. Other melodeons soon followed, like the Niagara Concert Hall on B Street and Sutliff's on C Street, which became the Virginia Music Hall in 1865. By November 1863, enough melodeon businesses existed for the city to charge a $250 a month licensing fee.

A quiet day in 1872 on Virginia City's main north–south thoroughfare, C Street. *UNRS-P1983-20-09, Nevada Photographs, Special Collections and University Archives Department, University of Nevada, Reno.*

Performers used a play on words in the dialogue or offered conundrums, a confusing or difficult question or observation, that would make the audience laugh. The miners in the audience could chuckle, snicker, sing along with the music, hoot and holler and forget for a few moments that they had to work underground, without sunlight, for much of their lives. Entertainment designed to make them happy included gambling tables and scantily-clad coy waitresses. They wanted to see performers and shows that validated their lived experiences, so many jokes supported working-class values.

In April 1863, Tom Maguire brought a touring company of minstrels from San Francisco to Topliffe's melodeon. Irish immigrant Tom Maguire found success in San Francisco after settling there in 1850 with other California

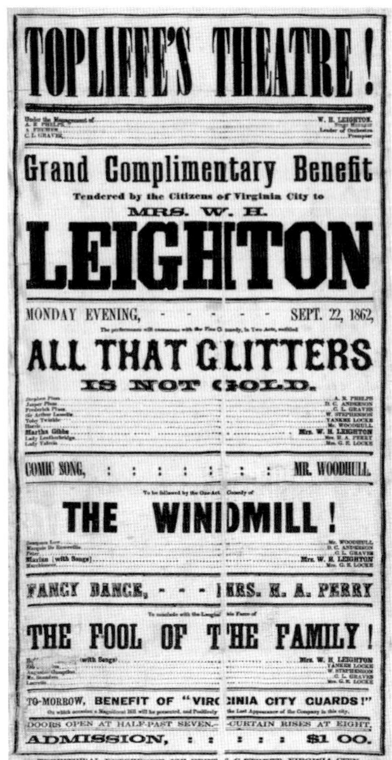

Left: Topliffe's opened July 4, 1862, changed ownership to the Virginia Melodeon in 1863 and was lost in a fire in August 1864. Notice the fancy dance by Mrs. H.A. Perry, who ended her theatrical career as Agnes Booth. *William C. Miller Papers, 87-06, Special Collection and University Archive Collection Department, University of Nevada, Reno.*

Right: Tom Maguire spent thirty years in the theatrical business in the West. *Center for Sacramento History.*

Gold Rush argonauts. Sharing his natal identity with many of the miners, Maguire felt he understood what men from his country would want to see in entertainment. He began to experiment with minstrelsy, already popular on the East Coast. Minstrel shows were based on comedy, music and singing and dancing and were performed in three-part presentations that featured a comedy sketch as the last act. Minstrel shows, geared toward nostalgia, bombarded the homesick miners with sentimental Irish ballads, jokes, elegant circumlocutions and riddles that reflected a shared Irish humor. Informal, improvisational, conversational, minstrel performers made up their material on the fly. The Irish immigrants in the audience had similarly suffered under English rule like Black Americans had under slavery, and the Irish embraced and appreciated the comedy performances by blackface comics, with whom they identified. They could relate to the humor and the deprecated status of the minstrels, who always seemed to get the best of the straight man—called the interlocutor—who was often presented in white face. But often, they made fun of people in ways that are not appreciated today, and the use of blackface enforced stereotypes of a lesser status for Black Americans.

Maguire built a theater in San Francisco as early as 1851 and then began by touring his minstrel troupes from the Bay City through the California Mother Lode mining camps of the 1850s. Soon, he added more legitimate performers in Shakespeare, classic plays and melodramas. He developed a circuit of towns where his performers could show their talents; from San Francisco, they traveled the delta waterways to Stockton, Sacramento and Marysville, also adding Grass Valley and Nevada City. He did not invent the circuit concept for touring actors, but he was the first western theater manager to employ the technique. Performers were constantly on the move, traveling a circuit of places to present their shows for people who would pay to see them and enjoy what they offered.

During his thirty-year managerial career Maguire built several theaters in California to showcase his performers. He built theaters in San Francisco, Sacramento and Marysville during the 1850s. Then in 1863, Tom Maguire built a rather large theater he called an opera house on the east side of D Street in Virginia City between Union and Taylor Streets. Maguire sent agents to the East Coast and even other countries to scout talent for his western theaters. He brought popular performers to Virginia City at a time when the town experienced such growth and enthusiasm that it was elevated to a status as the second most important city on the Pacific Coast behind only San Francisco.

One of Tom Maguire's theatrical strategies, seeking talent from other countries, brought Harry Courtaine and his wife to San Francisco in 1856. While there, Courtaine was jailed by Maguire in an attempt to sober him up. One account credited Maguire with imprisoning Courtaine for beating his wife. When Courtraine's fellow thespians bailed the comic out of jail, Maguire reprimanded the cast for spoiling his attempts to keep Courtaine sober. Harry Courtaine's graceful movements and beautiful singing onstage characterized the extremely versatile, great comic talent whose life embodied the pitfalls of the melodeon performer's reality. The comic spent twenty years on the West Coast, going from the stage to the gutter to the jail, where he even claimed a San Francisco cell was named for him. In the 1860s, Courtaine acted in Virginia City in various productions and then returned in 1871, when he joined the theater's supporting cast. He also became a

Comic actor Harry Courtaine. *California Historical Society, San Francisco.*

stage manager but worked in a hit-or-miss fashion, often failing to perform, supporting the tradition of his alcohol dependence. On January 9, 1872, the *Stockton Daily Herald* printed a notice that Harry Courtaine had been "sentenced to prison for three months as a common drunkard." Apparently able to remain sober for at least one year at a time, Courtaine returned to England from 1886 to 1888. Although he was earlier reported as deceased by a New York newspaper, Courtaine appeared in 1889 on the West Coast in *Little Puck* and other plays after experiencing a successful New York engagement. Ever popular with Western audiences, Courtaine played the original Maguire's Theater, became a manager under John Piper and then returned to perform in the extant theater for one night.

2

JAMES STARK

THE PIONEER ACTOR

[Mr. Stark's Iago] *was a subtle and powerful conception, artistically drawn in its general outline and more finished in its details than any delineation of the character that we remember to have ever witnessed.*
—believed the Territorial Enterprise *on April 27, 1869*

Fresh from successes on the East Coast, James Stark followed the masses in the California Gold Rush and brought a number of firsts to the West Coast as the first actor of prominence in both California and Nevada. He was credited with bringing serious drama to the Howard Street Theatre in Virginia City in November 1861. Then he became the opening act at Carson City's first theater and the first actor at the new Gold Hill Theater in May 1862, while also touring Silver City's Chrysopolis Hall and Dayton's Hall early on. As the first serious dramatic actor to take the far Western market seriously, James Stark embodied the pioneer, both in spirit and in performance history.

"Mr. Stark has a fine manly presence, good voice, and a bold, earnest, impassioned style," the *New York Herald* of April 6, 1858, noted. Stark brought legitimate drama—full-length plays, including Shakespearean works—to the West. Stark was also the first actor to pursue a political career there. While Stark's repertoire appealed to Western audiences, so, too, did his acting style. On the cusp of a change in nineteenth-century acting, Stark brought realism to the stage, eschewing the older, more bombastic, overwrought techniques of older stars.

Actor James Stark from a daguerreotype. *The Bancroft Library, University of California, Berkeley.*

Sacramento, where Stark began his Western career in 1850, created a jumping-off point for would-be miners who intended to find gold in the motherlode foothills of the Sierra Nevada. The town outfitted miners with necessities: tools, supplies and sustenance for their souls. Stark's *Damon and Pythias*, a classic story full of nineteenth-century values—honesty, trust, integrity and honor—carried a plot line that would remind men of their loyalty and responsibilities to their friends. Billed as "a test of friendship," the play finds Damon—Stark's favored role—in jail, trading places and trusting his friend to return and rescue him. When Pythias returns to face his punishment—death—the king frees both men, amazed at their mutual love and trust. Stark would continue to offer *Damon and Pythias* to Western audiences for the next eighteen years. Men comprised the overwhelming majority of the populations of some mining towns. Reinforcing proper values and behavior through entertainment created an environment of stability for miners who were uprooted from traditional family, friends and communities back home.

An actor's repertoire featured roles that showcased specific talents, endorsed societal values and satisfied audience expectations. Shakespeare, revered by both audiences and actors, understood that the universal human emotions and frailties depicted in his plays spoke to audience members through plots laced with tension and intrigue. Love, lust, power, pride, jealousy, fate, ambition and indecision over enduring battles of right and wrong kept theatergoers on the edge of their seats. Stark kept to the original text of Shakespeare, a tactic that aided his audience acceptance. A versatile actor, he is credited with being the first in the West to play several roles, including Shakespeare's Hamlet, Brutus, Falstaff and Petruchio. Often considered Stark's signature role, the crafty, obstreperous cardinal Richelieu was believed by some to be his best impersonation. Richelieu is a well-written character study that when performed by many actors as a mumbling, kindly, tenderhearted guardian found his thoughts and moods could be illuminated by his constant mutterings. "Faultless in his delineation of most characters," constituted high praise of Stark from the *Territorial Enterprise*.

Stark managed Sacramento's Tehama Theater in a sizzling partnership with high-strung actress Sarah Kirby, whom he married. They gave San Francisco its first successful dramatic season. Roughly six years older than handsome Stark, Sarah was the first actress to take men's roles in the West, the first to use publicity to bolster actors' celebrity and the first female theater manager in the West.

Sarah Stark, pictured in her later years. She was a "first" in many roles in the West, including the first female theater manager. *The Bancroft Library, University of California, Berkeley.*

By 1845, Sarah had taken leading roles in New York City before she subsequently moved west. Her best roles were the titular *Lady of Lyons* and Lady Macbeth, and she was known for depicting a range of emotions from indignant scorn and injured virtue to flirtatious charm. Together, James and Sarah Stark should be credited with raising the standard of drama in the West. Toward the end of 1863, Sarah began a partnership with actress Emily Jordan in management of San Francisco's Metropolitan Theater, which did not last more than a year.

Born into a theatrical family, Emily Jordan was considered one of the most beautiful actresses in the West during the height of her career in the 1860s. She performed at Maguire's Virginia City Opera House in October 1864 in several challenging roles, including the outcast Leah in *Leah the Forsaken* and *Mazeppa*, only a few months after the great Adah Isaacs Menken. She left that engagement early after a scathing review in the *Enterprise* accused her of showing her legs rather than her ability and pointed out that she needed to blow her nose.

James and Sarah Stark enjoyed success during the first years of the 1850s, as the Gold Rush brought hordes of people to the West. When the first blush of gold hysteria ended by 1853, mining declined. The following year the West slid into an economic depression. Driven by reports of a new gold rush and seeking wealthy audiences, the Starks left San Francisco for Australia, becoming the first American actors to perform there. This 1853 tour reportedly netted the Starks $100,000. Not surprisingly, they returned down under in 1856. Although Mrs. Stark stirred up trouble by suggesting that good press reviews could be bought for a £5 note, the addition of the controversial play *Camille*, about a courtesan with a heart of gold, garnered Sarah well-deserved praise for her acting. The dying coquette silenced the house when her grief and resignation "so bordered on reality as to become almost painful to witness," according to an Australian newspaper. She would later become the first actress to attempt *Camille* in Virginia City.

The Starks' tours in 1859 included Oregon and British Columbia, another gold rush region, and they became the first American actors to bring legitimate drama to Southern California. A fifty-night engagement in San Francisco earned Stark the sobriquet "California's favorite actor."

In late 1861, Stark completed a tour through the booming Nevada towns of Virginia City and Carson City, becoming the first prominent dramatic actor in this new region as well. In Virginia City, the machinery for hoisting the drop curtain failed, drawing jeers from the audience. "Haul away on that mainsheet you lubbers!" they yelled at stagehands who were trying to fix the problem curtain, as reported in the local paper. Stark then opened the first Carson City theater behind a bar room where a local band preferred to play "Dixie" over "Yankee Doodle," showing a disturbing preference for the Confederacy. Even with these missteps in the dramatic world, Stark regretted only the horse-drawn stage trip from Virginia City to Placerville—which lasted three days—as the roughest part of the adventure. It exceeded in "rugged interest" anything else he had experienced in his travel in the West. Undeterred, he returned to Nevada within six months, opening the small Gold Hill Theater with his own Star Dramatic Company. Then he played Topliffe's in July 1862 within a few weeks of its opening.

In 1862, James Stark moved permanently to Nevada Territory to embark on a mining career in Aurora. His relocation hinged on a letter that Sam Clemens—who, in 1863, became Mark Twain—wrote to his brother Orion, the secretary of Nevada Territory. Both Stark and Clemens held optimistic mining interests on Last Chance Hill. Aurora experienced two dozen violent deaths in its first three years, along with fires, shootings and visits from vigilantes. Stark reported that there were insufficient men to fill the jobs available and silver veins "fine, wide, and rich" flourished. "Saloons—saloons—saloons—liquor everywhere…gambling and vice in all its horrible realities," observed William Brewer. Like the aurora borealis shining above, the town bloomed rapidly and then passed into obscurity.

In Aurora, the tragedian gave ten theatrical readings but grew bored and turned his attention to politics. In September 1863, Stark was elected to represent Esmeralda County at the Nevada Constitutional Convention. The group was tasked with writing a state constitution, which was a framework of government needed to achieve statehood. This first convention's constitution did not pass, but it created a template for the final document.

As the Civil War raged in the East, the conventioneers faced an immense question: Would the treasonous Confederates be allowed to vote in Nevada? America's founding fathers had not foreseen such struggles, Stark avowed. Men "rather lukewarm" about treason, forced Stark to argue, "We are justified in our attempts to strengthen what we consider…weak…on this vital question."

Sam Clemens, who lived in Aurora from April to September 1862, reported on the convention for the *Territorial Enterprise*, reprinted in the *New York Clipper* and other newspapers. The *Enterprise* wrote: "In view of the great oratorical powers of Mr. Stark as we have listened to them on many a stage, and the fervor, elegance and patriotism of the speech itself, we pronounce it one of the best specimens of eloquence ever delivered…among the classical models of our language." Most probably it was Clemens, who then gave "a taste of his quality":

> *Why sir, to my mind (and my soul sickens at its contemplation) treason is a crime of such awful magnitude that there is not adequate punishment on this earth for it; thus, like the sin against the Holy Ghost—it is the Unpardonable Crime! Sir, for its punishment justice calls aloud from every battle-field in our once peaceful and happy country. We hear it in every widow's shriek of despair; in every father's cry of anguish; in every loyal son's demand for vengeance; in every daughter's moan for all her pure young heart, held most dear and sacred. What terms of reprobation can speak our abhorrence of this crime. O, for a tongue of fire and lips of flame to imprint upon all loyal hearts the necessity of that watchful vigilance which alone can guard our liberties.*

We can hear the tragedian's voice rise to a crescendo: "What terms of reprobation can I utter against the instigators of this rebellion? Sir, language fails me to express it. Oh, is there not some chosen curse—some thunderbolt, red with uncommon wrath—to strike the bold usurper down who builds his greatness on his country's ruin!" Stark was as powerful in politics as he was on the stage. The *Enterprise* felt Stark held "a place in the hearts of the people…of Nevada" and found him sincere. The day following Stark's "flaming, patriotic" speech convention members voted to limit speeches, but also retained passages that Stark championed, ensuring "paramount allegiance" to the federal government by every citizen. It became a repudiation of the Confederacy's states' rights doctrines.

Stark's political career carried a backstory. When Stark performed in Carson City, his theater scenery was torn and ransacked by a Copperhead, a term for a southern sympathizer. This man reportedly killed another and attacked the pro-Union Stark and members of his cast. Incidents like these brought home the polarized political reality of the Civil War.

From 1864 through 1867, Stark performed in grueling tours across the country, as did other actors who headed west. Stark became the first legitimate actor to play Cheyenne, Wyoming, in 1867 during these tours. Sarah Stark stayed in California during most of these adventures, as the Starks' marriage ultimately dissolved in 1866. Sarah divorced him alleging his infidelity with a widow, Phoebe Smith, a charming beauty more than twenty years his junior.

Back home by 1869, Stark joined a theatrical company bound for Nevada. During Stark's performance in *Hamlet*'s first act, he suffered a nosebleed significant enough to be noticed by the audience. Blamed on Virginia City's high elevation, the nosebleed heralded worse things to come. Stark was struck with a series of strokes that left him completely paralyzed on his right side. Unable to speak for two months, he lingered at the International Hotel. The money he received from benefit donations allowed Stark and Phoebe to return to New York, where he suffered a stroke from which he never fully recovered. He appeared in only minor roles until his death in 1875, aided by other actors who sympathized with his plight.

"An admirable actor," "kind and generous," said newspapers. James Stark's place in Western history is driven by firsts; he was the first dramatic tragedian in the West, the first American actor to tour Australia and the first Western actor to become a politician, driven by integrity and concern over America's future. One critic ranked him with only four other contemporary actors as among the best; while another felt he was second to none. His position as an actor of genius had been attained only after great struggles, and "in nobility of personal character," he was "inferior to no citizen of the country," reported California newspapers.

Louise Arnot started as a child actress with the Marsh Family Troupe. *Author's collection.*

Stark costarred with many fine actresses during his long career, including Nellie

The International Hotel frequently lodged visiting actors. *Society of California Pioneers.*

Brown and Virginia Howard in Virginia City at Maguire's Opera House. One of Stark's costars, Louise Arnot, had performed since childhood. Beginning with the Marsh Troupe at Maguire's 1863 theater, she enjoyed a sixty-year stage career. Arnot experienced more freedom and autonomy than most women of her day. She represents one of a large group of actresses who trained on Virginia City's stages and then went on to long successful careers. Statuesque, with a deep voice, she played leading male characters beginning at the age of twelve. In 1869, *Henry IV*, a first in Virginia City, found interesting casting, with Louise Arnot in the male role of Sir Richard Vernon, opposite John McCullough and James Stark, who executed the leads.

3

MAGUIRE'S OPERA HOUSE

DRINKS, DRAMA AND D STREET

They were mostly made up of great bearded fellows, in rough clothing and cowhide boots, who carried their bags of gold dust with them.
—actress Pauline Markham referring to the audience,
New York Dramatic Mirror, *October 23, 1897*

Irish immigrant Tom Maguire worked as a bartender in an upstairs bar at New York's Park Theater, where he learned the theater business that tied him to audiences of working people. Why change something that had previously succeeded? Maguire followed the Forty-Niners—people who headed west for the California Gold Rush—to San Francisco, where he established several theaters and became a major theatrical manager until the early 1880s. In San Francisco, Maguire first established a saloon and then built the Jenny Lind Theater, named for a star who never visited. Maguire also championed the theatrical circuit, which capitalized on the geographic expanse of settlement in the West. He soon built theaters in the California interior towns of Marysville and Sacramento, where he could showcase his San Francisco performers. In 1863, he built Maguire's Opera House in Virginia City. It was three stories high with a judicial court and a jail on lower levels on the E Street side. Actress Pauline Markham recalled having to walk over the jail cells when entering the stage. The prisoners reached up through the bars and attempted to grab her legs. She said, "But there were compensations for these little inconveniences. The audiences had plenty of money which they spent freely, and they were very appreciative," reported the *Mirror*.

In the post–Civil War decade, immigrant businessmen dominated the Western theatrical landscape, with Thomas Maguire controlling the important theaters of California and Nevada with the building of his opera house in Virginia City. He became the most prominent theatrical manager in the American West, often called the "Napoleon" of managers. Shrewd—a businessman, not an actor—Maguire created a plethora of theatrical assets that foreshadowed the theatrical syndicates of the late 1800s. Maguire's San Francisco theaters dominated the theatrical life of the area for fifteen years prior to the building of the California Theater, which, after 1869, would eclipse Maguire's locations as the prominent venue for legitimate theater—melodramas, classic plays and Shakespeare. Maguire's business model of alternating attractions at his theaters, building theaters devoted to different types of entertainment (thus drawing different audiences), bringing in recognized "stars" and attempting to maintain a good stock company of backup supporting cast members while taking troupes on tour were all factors in his success.

The stock company, or supporting players, excelled in versatile shifts from comedy to pathos, singing and dancing and anything else required to help create a finished entertainment experience. English actor Edmund Leathes recalled being offered a part at 11:30 a.m. that he was expected to present that evening. Ingeniously, he tore a page of the script from his playbook and inserted it into the interior crown of his hat. With a flourish, he could then remove the hat and read the speech pasted inside. While hardly a finished performance, it was an expeditious solution.

The abundance of dramatic fare presented by the actors is nearly beyond modern comprehension, as the plays changed almost nightly, and a starring player had at least thirty major roles at their disposal. In some ways, the 1860s became the theater's golden era, characterized by large repertoires of memorized plays for each actor working in the supporting stock companies. The stock players had a repertoire of plays to use in the absence of a star, and the reputation of a theater's stock company influenced an actor's decision about performing in that theater. These supporting companies generally had various players who followed their "line of business," such as old man, old woman, soubrette and low comedian, for whatever play appeared before the audience. Both stock companies and lines of business died out by the 1880s.

The "spacious and beautiful" theater that Maguire built in Virginia City copied his San Francisco Opera House "exactly," according to author Mark Twain. Maguire's Opera House had three levels on its E Street side because of the distinctive slope of the mountain town and two stories on its D Street

The second building on the right was Maguire's Opera House on D Street, 1865. Notice the balcony where the band played. *The Bancroft Library, University of California, Berkeley.*

side with an entrance for respectable folks accessible through a saloon. The Opera House enjoyed a 50-foot-wide frontage on D Street and 150 feet in depth. Because of the steep slope, the second floor, on E Street, featured a balcony on stilts, with about a 15-foot drop to the earth below. Nearly one-thousand people could sit comfortably in Maguire's Opera House to watch any number of plays and performers previously booked into his San Francisco theaters and now on tour. The Opera House opened on July 2, 1863, with a comedy play called *Money*. The beautiful and "manly" theater survived a severe storm on opening night when it "creaked in the tempest like a ship at sea," according to actor Walter Leman.

The theater on D Street opened only two months before the city aldermen created a legal red-light district on D Street north of the Union cross street. Women who exchanged sexual favors for money were supposed to be confined to that area, and indeed, cribs, or small houses, developed along that corridor to house the women. Another area, the Barbary Coast on lower C Street, also developed, although ordinance enforcement personnel generally ignored infractions. Women who exchanged sexual favors for money would frequent the theater in large numbers and become significant financial support to the business.

Upstairs, seating for the "fallen women" of D Street was facilitated by a staircase from the street level to a door that led directly to the boxes. The women were considered so dishonorable that they could not enter the front door with the respectable patrons. To keep them segregated, the women were relegated to their own accommodations, including a separate saloon, behind heavily curtained boxes on the second level of Maguire's Opera House. This segregation of fallen women followed the architecture of Maguire's San Francisco Jenny Lind Theater and the Park Theater, where he had worked in New York, and it reflected society's beliefs at the time: out of sight, out of mind. Boxes with heavy curtains allowed the occupants to maintain a bit of privacy for their trysts. Maguire's Opera House had a balcony where the theater's little band—usually only three or four musicians—played before a show to let the townsfolk know that there would be entertainment in the theater that night. An upstairs gallery offered cheap seats, while the dress circle seats went for one dollar or more, a significant amount of money in the 1860s.

Respectable patrons were greeted by pictures of Maggie Moore and Lotta Crabtree upon entrance. Both women excelled in performing songs, dances and minstrelsy. Waiter girls served drinks to the crowd, but over time, a reduction in the number of waitresses was noted when legitimate dramas drew respectable women to the theater. Challenges to morality were also noted with the green room. While these spaces are traditionally resting spots for performers between acts, Maguire's green room allowed audience members to visit with performers, presumably facilitating liaisons. In late 1867, a new and convenient actor's green room, open to theater patrons, was built on the north side of the theater building, with a door that opened onto a piazza on D Street.

Maggie Moore, born Margaret Sullivan in San Francisco, was always considered a local favorite. She performed in minstrel shows in Virginia City and had a dancing act with her brother starting in 1866. A member of Maguire's San Francisco Minstrels, then his California Minstrels, Maggie became a fixture in his theaters. She eventually progressed to dramatic plays by the 1870s, returning to Virginia City in 1871 as a supporting company player. She signed a one-year contract with McCullough's California Theater as a soubrette, debuting there in late 1872.

The theater's interior, based on the memoir of an actress who played Virginia City in the early 1870s, shows a lively, festive space. *Internet Archive.*

Maguire found appreciative audiences among the working classes of the mining towns and built his success on fulfilling their needs—both with entertainment on stage and "entertainment" in the boxes. Maguire opened his Virginia City Opera House, a title presumed to give more prestige and respectability to a theater, with a troupe including Frank Mayo. A second-generation Irishman, Mayo, like Maguire, had come west for the Gold Rush. After experiencing poor luck as a miner, Mayo drifted toward Maguire's theatrical establishments and learned the ropes. Mayo attempted *Hamlet* in Virginia City, his first execution of that role, as a special request from Virginia City's business elite. Many had tired of the sensuous variety theaters' entertainment—three competing melodeons when Maguire's opened in 1863—and wanted more respectable full-length plays in the newly built Opera House. The tensions between respectability and the more lucrative sensational programming for miners would continue throughout Virginia City's theatrical history.

Boston-born Frank Mayo took backstage jobs with Tom Maguire's theaters until he moved into performing, using western theaters as a training ground for East Coast theaters. Eventually, he became one of the most respected Victorian-era American actors, with a celebrated forty-year career. His successful leading role in *The Streets of New York* was exhaustively staged in Virginia City in 1870 for a six-night engagement. *The Streets of New York* featured thrilling action, tenement fires and real firefighting equipment dragged onstage by a horse—all supported by actress Sue Robinson. Later successes included *Davy Crockett*, *Nordeck*, and *Puddin'head Wilson* among others.

The most successful actors were featured in tobacco card advertisements, such as this one of Maggie Moore. *Author's collection.*

Frank Mayo is an example of one of the many actors who learned his craft on Western stages and then parlayed that skill to stages in New York City and elsewhere. The famous Booths, father Junius Brutus Booth, along with Edwin and June Jr., came west during the 1850s, allowing Mayo to study their techniques at Maguire's theaters. Mayo's leading man duties opposite Adah Isaacs Menken in San Francisco, brought him notoriety. Traveling to New York in 1869, he accepted a salary bested by only one other actor. He toured for much of his life in *Davy Crockett.*

To be in the stock company of an 1860s theater took a much higher standard of ability and a much wider repertoire to reach success than in later years. Maguire's fine

Frank Mayo costumed for a Shakespearean role. *Author's collection.*

supporting cast included Walter Leman and Elizabeth Saunders, who both lasted in the profession for years, performing in Virginia City many times. In 1878, San Francisco celebrated the character actor Leman's over fifty years in the profession. Saunders frequently traveled to Maguire's hinterland theaters in support of numerous stars and appeared in Virginia City as late as 1879. Also a member of the California Theater stock company, she acted into the 1880s.

Tom Maguire owned his Virginia City Opera House from 1863 to 1867, experiencing four years of middling successes from his stock company of players and independent touring actors and actresses. One name stands out: Adah Isaacs Menken. Menken's one-month engagement became, arguably, Maguire's greatest success in Virginia City. Her unconventional creations filled Maguire's theater in San Francisco where she brought in a record $4,700 in only three nights. Her most beloved and controversial role as the Tartar prince in *Mazeppa* set western audiences in a tizzy. Menken, as the Prince, transcended boundaries with transgressive behavior: performing as a man while wearing scanty, body-revealing clothing. In the play's most acclaimed scene, Menken was dressed in white or flesh-colored tights and gossamer fabric, tied to the side of a horse that climbed a wooden platform and ramps that were placed onstage to simulate mountainous terrain.

Stereotypes of actresses as unconventional grew from women such as Menken trying to control their own public persona. Menken wrote to newspapermen—she called them her "pals"—to get her name in the papers. She relished stories of her private life escaping as exciting scandalous activities. It kept her name before the public and kept the public paying at the theater doors for entry to her shows. Menken's legacy lay with her ascendancy and encouragement of the star system, as she purposefully created a celebrity status for herself through her own promotions.

Tom Maguire's Virginia City Opera House was not his most successful. Factors beyond his control included recessions in mining production due to technological inadequacies and a contentious lawsuit with a business partner. Also, Maguire failed to properly befriend the local newspapermen who held the power of critical reviews. Moreover, unanticipated deaths,

Opposite: Walter Leman was one of the first actors to appear at Maguire's Opera House when it opened in 1863, writing the dedication speech for the facility. *Internet Archive.*

Right: Mrs. Elizabeth Saunders was a stock company player for Tom Maguire for many years, coming to San Francisco in 1850 and first performing in 1852. She toured Virginia City many times. *Author's collection.*

one of a theater manager and one of a lessee, spelled doom. Tom Peasley, a sometime lawman and local sport, partnered with a local blacksmith and leased the theater from Maguire in late 1865. Death took Peasley in February the following year. He was shot and killed in a Carson City saloon. While dying, he raised his gun at the last moment to shoot his assailant in a double murder. The losses foreshadowed Maguire's sale of the business.

Tom Maguire retired in 1882 after his involvement with thirteen theaters in the West. His greatest mistakes were failing to read the audience, underestimating respectable women as patrons, and failing to adapt to new approaches and changes within the greater culture. He was successful when fallen women needed the theater as a place of assignation but failed when respectable women needed to find solace in the voices of strong actresses who presented dramatic plays based on topics of interest to their concerns. He was sued for discrimination by Black patrons when he refused to seat

Adah Isaacs Menken was wildly transgressive by Victorian standards, frequenting Virginia City's saloons where respectable women dared not tread. *Author's collection.*

them in preferred areas; factors that characterize Maguire as a person stuck in the past with a failure to change with societal advancements.

To survive in the theater business in Virginia City, cultural paradigms needed to be respected. It was necessary to value entrenched notions about class and gender, but also necessary to value the Victorian ideals of respectability. Survival required innovation in providing a theater experience acceptable to all patrons. The most expensive seats in the dress circle found respectable women in attendance—but only when escorted by a man. What then appeared onstage needed to not offend or embarrass.

4

THE PIPER BROTHERS TAKE CHARGE

[John and Henry Piper] *have their mammoth yellow posters "up" for their melodeon. They have secured a row of talent such as can't be overcome on this coast.*
—*observed the* Gold Hill Daily News, *October 7, 1867*

John Piper and his two younger brothers, Joachim (later Joseph) and Heindrick (later Henry), born in Fisherhude, Germany, immigrated to San Francisco in the 1850s in lieu of serving in the German military, according to the memories of Henry's son. John established a fruit stand and liquor business in San Francisco near a notorious variety theater, the Bella Union. Undoubtedly, he learned of the potential profits to be made in the theater world.

Upon settling in Virginia City, John established a saloon at the corner of B and Union Streets, which became one of the longest continuously operating saloons of the nineteenth century in Virginia City. Advertisements in the *Territorial Enterprise* newspaper for the Old Corner Saloon date to as early as 1861, with John Piper as proprietor. By the early 1860s, John lived in an apartment over his saloon at 1 North B Street on the northwest corner of the intersection, as one of the largest landowners of the town. Houses of ill fame were built near the saloon property, and early reporting on a fire show Piper owned several in the area.

Henry clerked in John's San Francisco grocery business and worked as a bartender or assistant in the new Virginia City saloon business. The saloon itself enjoyed infamy due to its clientele, including Mark Twain. The author lived in Virginia City from September 1862 to May 1864; his story is told in

San Francisco's Bella Union variety theater was run like a brothel, according to an early manager. John Piper established a grocery and liquor business next door. *Museum of Performance and Design, San Francisco, CA.*

Left: John Piper, born in 1830, died in 1897 after thirty years in the theater business. He is the foremost theater manager in Nevada's history. *California Historical Society, San Francisco, CA.*

Right: Henry Piper, John's youngest brother, partnered with him in the theater and saloon businesses. *Special Collections Photographs, UNRS-P0182-1.tif collection_6505; Special Collection and University Archive Collection department, University of Nevada, Reno.*

many other places. Piper's saloon on B Street is specifically mentioned in an article in the *Eureka Daily Sentinel* of May 1877 as the local haunt of Samuel Clemens and other "Bohemians" during his sojourn with the *Territorial Enterprise* newspaper. Located only a few steps away from the *Enterprise* office on C Street, the office had a staircase to the higher B Street that facilitated a quick jaunt to Piper's saloon across the street.

When actors managed their own theaters, they equated success with better plays, better actors and better scenery or special effects—all ideas related to the concept that what was presented onstage was art. To both Maguire and Piper, money typified the important motivation; theater was a business similar to others. Both men may have been similarly motivated to invest in the theater businesses because of their knowledge of the lucrative audiences of working women who used theaters as places to meet clients. Piper emulated some of Maguire's strategies, including touring plays to neighboring towns and employing good actors in the stock company. He also used strategies that included buying competitive saloon theaters—at least two during his early years of operation—and establishing relationships with theaters in San

Francisco. As the leading theatrical center on the West Coast, San Francisco had numerous melodeon businesses, most primarily located along the city's notorious Barbary Coast, as well as theaters devoted to legitimate drama and the classics. Piper drew performers from both the best theaters and the melodeons to consistently bring talent to the mining town.

A strong connection to geography influenced Virginia City's location on the east–west transportation network and benefitted the theater by supplying performers who were going to or coming from San Francisco. When the Pipers took over Tom Maguire's theater business in 1867, the transcontinental railroad had not yet been completed. People used the overland route in wagons or stagecoaches, and coaches serviced the route from Reno to Virginia City. Freight wagons brought necessities into town, and ore hauled to the mills passed through with twelve- to fourteen-horse or mule teams. The settlement perched on the hillside claimed a few thousand souls, many of them, like the Pipers, were immigrants.

When he purchased the theater in March 1867, John Piper immediately began making improvements, adding two large heating stoves, gas lights and weatherboarding to the original Maguire's Opera House to make it more comfortable for patrons. Even with the new siding, the theater subjected actors to snow blowing in through gaps in its walls, creating teeth-chattering winter conditions. Gas light replaced the more dangerous coal oil. Gas lighting was crucial to the success of plays and had been introduced to American theaters as early as 1816. The upstage region of the stage, illuminated by gas light, allowed actors to physically move upstage to perform within the scenery, not just in front of it. Burning buildings, volcanoes and other special effects required gas to reach full dramatic potential. Piper also changed the entrance to the theater. Then he added ten box seats, five at either side of the dress circle, and expanded an entrance from the side of the theater to the dress circle, making it "comfortable" and "convenient," according to the *Gold Hill News*. The *Daily Trespass* believed this made it desirable for a melodeon business, allowing for the conclusion that the boxes allowed fallen women to offer sexual favors therein.

Indeed, early newspaper advertisements called Piper's Opera House a melodeon. The fact that the *Daily Trespass* noted the melodeon nature of the programming—sexually stimulating costuming and dialogue—suggested a large portion of the clientele came from the nascent red-light district, a short walk down D Street. The boxes enabled discrete encounters between the largely single male population and the working women of the town. The addition of more boxes and a drop in ticket prices from ten dollars per box, started in 1863 by Maguire, argues for the importance of these women to the theater business' financial success and the desire to cultivate their patronage.

Piper's goal was simple: make money. But his own lack of experience in theatrical matters caused him to rent out the theater to Max Walter. Walter had previously run his own San Francisco Music Hall for a month until it was closed by the more respectable members of the community, who found it a challenge to morality. Walter then moved on to Sutliffe's Melodeon on C Street with an entry on D Street. Known for Tableau Vivants—women in scanty clothing standing as statues on stage as visual enticement for men—Walter continued as the proprietor when the melodeon became the Virginia Music Hall. Sutliffe's had opened in December 1863, but after the building's demise in a rousing fire in 1866, Walter leased Tom Maguire's Virginia City theater prior to the Pipers' takeover. Then Walter continued management of the theater under the Piper brothers after their purchase. Perhaps remembering Harry Courtaine's stint at the melodeon, the *Gold Hill News* touted Walter always gave "better shows than anyone who has ever made the attempt." But challenges from the respectable community made Walter's new tenure short-lived. Walter's big problem? He failed to keep the fallen women confined to the theater boxes and let them mix with the respectable folk in the dress circle.

John Piper, Virginia City's mayor at the time of his purchase of the Opera House, did not gain his party's endorsement for reelection. The local newspapers agreed in their condemnation of Walter's management. They huffed about fallen women seated in the dress circle. Why weren't they told of this policy? The subsequent brouhaha in the local newspapers spilled over to Piper's political failures. Undoubtedly, he learned a lesson on the importance of the newspaper's coverage of the theater. In September 1867, John and his brother Henry partnered to run the new Piper's Opera House. Newspaper articles document this partnership, and deeds of the early 1870s show that ownership of the Opera House property on D Street passed back and forth between John and Henry. They consistently advertised in the local papers.

Little is reported in local newspapers of Henry's work in support of the Opera House, but it can be determined that Henry was a bartender and a box herder. While Henry worked in the Opera House in November 1867, a dispute between two performers over earrings resulted in a burlesque of the event being performed as part of a minstrel show. As the event had occurred in the saloon of the Opera House, Henry may have been presiding over the bar at the time of the dispute. Later reporting allows for the conclusion

Pictured are actresses Amy Stone (*left*) and Alice Kingsbury. *Special Collections Photographs, UNRS-P1326-1.tif collection_6449; Special Collection and University Archive Collection Department, University of Nevada, Reno.*

that Henry became the "box herder," a management function primarily concerned with keeping the peace—and perhaps keeping the curtains closed on the theater boxes used for rendezvous.

Both Amy Stone and Alice Kingsbury performed in 1867 at Piper's Opera House. Stone performed a long engagement and then returned for many years, including 1869 and 1874. In April 1869, the worst single disaster in Comstock history, the Yellow Jacket Mine fire, struck during an engagement by Amy Stone. Her benefit performances to aid the lost miners' families made her a local favorite. Like other actresses, she developed and managed her own touring company, primarily performing in popular melodramas. Melodramas include a heroine, a hero and a villain. Plots could be simple or highly circuitous, but by the end of the play, good always prevails and evil is vanquished.

Alice Kingsbury had toured the United States during the 1860s and made a second appearance in October 1866 at Maguire's San Francisco Opera House, where she received praise for her versatility with light comedy as well as "the more pathetic" roles. While there, Miss Kingsbury volunteered to teach a Sunday school class at a local Baptist church. The *Sacramento Daily Union* reported,

> *The offer was accepted and the Superintendent complimented the lady on the manner in which she performed the duties. He, however, when lecturing to the children on their duties, warned them to shun the theater, for it was "a lighthouse of hell, and all the actors and actresses were emissaries of the devil." Cognizant of the challenges to respectability that Victorian actors faced, Miss Kingsbury got up and said she was an actress and a member of the church, and in a short speech defended the profession in a manner that placed* hors du combat *the man who had opened the war.*

Many other actresses were noteworthy in their reticence to play on the Sabbath, and some attended any one of Virginia City's many churches while playing the mining town. Miss Kingsbury remained a defendant of the theatrical profession and a feminist as she moved into a writing career after her best years as an actress ended. Her signature leading role in *Fanchon, the Cricket* is one she played until her announced final performance in 1891 and then her final, final performance in 1892.

The *Territorial Enterprise* accused the California papers of overrating Kingsbury's abilities while the *Gold Hill News* found her style "simple" and "natural." Her *Child of the Savannah,* while attacked by the *Enterprise* as a "dramatic debauch," was greeted with such adulation from the audience that a commemorative poem written by a local man appeared in the paper. The *Trespass* explained that the audience included people of "vitiated tastes." There were audience members who "would have sworn that a naked Menken was more to be admired than the refined, intellectual, yet artless [Kingsbury]."

A mid-May benefit found Alice Kingsbury as Parthenia in *Ingomar, the Barbarian*, starring alongside John McCullough. *Ingomar* was an older romantic melodrama that had premiered in New York in 1851. Destined to be played in Virginia City on many occasions, the beauty-and-the-beast story witnessed the leading lady win over the leader of invading barbarians. The play is famous for the lines that end the second act: "Two souls with but a single thought; Two hearts that beat as one." Gold Hill newspaperman

John McCullough as Spartacus in *The Gladiator*, one of his most acclaimed roles. *Internet Archive*.

Alf Doten took his mistress, Mrs. M, and his dog Kyser to see the play with him. Kyser apparently appreciated the play more than many of the human audience members. According to Doten, the dog didn't know what to make of the cast dressed in animal skins, "such queer looking beasts." Regardless of Kingsbury's offerings of *The Robbers*, *Lady of Lyons* or *Fanchon*, in Virginia City, crowds attended to see McCullough, as his *Richard III* was offered to an "overflowing audience" and his *Hamlet* was "far better performed than ever before in this state." The *Enterprise* continued its exuberant belief that McCullough could "create a healthy demand for the standard drama."

John McCullough practiced on Virginia City stages and then starred in San Francisco and eventually became one of the most celebrated Victorian-era American actors. The *Boston Herald* of January 16, 1883, issued a tribute to McCullough that included, "McCullough has cultivated that evenness of style which is the true criterion of what is best in the actor's art. There is probably no tragedian on the stage today more capable of bursting into moments of fury, electrifying passion if he chose; but recognizing the fact that there are other and better things to accomplish, and that 'still waters run deep.'"

Although John McCullough is the best example, many other players were able to use Piper's Opera House as a training ground for the development of their craft to go on to acclaimed careers in San Francisco—some even experienced success nationally and internationally. Handsome, genial John McCullough first journeyed west in 1866 in the employ of his mentor Edwin Forrest, one of the foremost American actors of the antebellum era. When Forrest returned to the East Coast, McCullough stayed, taking stock company roles in San Francisco. By mid-1867, he secured a six-week engagement at Piper's Opera House, starring with Kingsbury. Here, he first performed

Left: Fanny Hanks. *Special Collections Photographs, UNRS-P1267-1.tif collection_6476, Special Collection and University Archive Collection Department, University of Nevada, Reno.*

Right: Kathleen O'Neill performed as Kitty From Cork. *Special Collections Photographs, UNRS-P1306-1.tif collection_6539; Special Collection and University Archive Collection Department, University of Nevada, Reno.*

the roles that became the cornerstone of his repertoire for the remainder of his career. Although he contended with diminishing audiences, as they were drawn to a new local melodeon called the Black Crook, McCullough received the attention of respectable folk, in part through the exceptionally positive reviews likely written by Dan DeQuille for the *Territorial Enterprise*. McCullough repeatedly returned to become a local favorite, and in 1868, he played opposite the nationally known Lawrence Barrett because of a $500 bonus. Eventually, McCullough used his Western successes to become one the most admired nineteenth-century American tragedians.

With praise for McCullough, the Piper brothers began to see the benefit of appealing to the town's more elevated people. Local newspaper advertisements specifically listed box seating prices so that the D Street women would be relegated to their own status location. Also, John Piper began a pattern he continued for the remainder of his days as theater manager; he traveled to San Francisco to bring back the best performers.

Two important female variety stars, Fanny Hanks and Kitty from Cork, began long engagements in October 1867. They were among the first performers under Piper's new management. Fanny Hanks remained a supporting company member from late 1867 until July 2, 1868, when she took her specialties, including the recitation of "Sheridan's Ride," about the Irish Civil War General Sheridan, back to California. During this time, she supported touring dramatic offerings and played interludes and melodeon nights. Expectations ran high, as performers were required to successfully present classic dramas, schmaltzy melodramas, songs, dances and comic readings. They were even expected to master one or more musical instruments. Hanks was named by fellow minstrel player Joe Taylor as one of "the best available talents on the coast at that time," often considered the best clog dancer. Similar to modern tap, clog dancing was brought to America by Irish immigrants. Virginia City's local firefighters concurred with Taylor and awarded Fanny Hanks an honorary membership in Engine Company No. 1.

Although she was born in Dublin, Kathleen "Kitty" O'Neill billed herself as Kitty from Cork. She used her thick Irish brogue to bring homesick Irish immigrants some respite in America. With Fanny Hanks, Kitty elevated the quality of performance for Piper in his earliest days as theater manager, thus giving him the opportunity to drive his competition—the Black Crook Melodeon—into bankruptcy.

5

1868

A BOOM YEAR BRINGS BIG STARS

What glorious nerves that woman must have!
—a reviewer noted in the Daily Alta California, *June 3, 1868,*
after watching the reaction of an actress to a Virginia City earthquake

At Piper's Opera House 1868 was a banner year, as the use of the recently developed dynamite gave an advantage to the mining enterprises that then thrived in Virginia City. People prospered and spent disposable income on the theater. There were few nights without a performance, and many luminaries appeared. Lawrence Barrett had been recruited by Tom Maguire to perform in San Francisco, and then subsequently recruited by John Piper for a three-week run in Virginia City. Barrett vied with Edwin Booth on the national hierarchy of "best" actors to become one of the most acclaimed actors in the role of Hamlet for the Victorian era, often considered the best role he executed. One historian noted that Barrett had performed every role in *Hamlet* except Polonius and the first grave digger. This was Barrett's first of five engagements in Virginia City, including those in 1870, 1872, 1875 and 1879. Barrett and McCullough became among the best actors of the nineteenth century to repeatedly perform in the West. But Barrett lacked McCullough's charm and always struggled against the common tropes of masculinity that credited the taller, handsome McCullough with greater respect. Additionally, McCullough was generous, warm and open-hearted with

Lawrence Barrett eventually became one of the wealthiest actors in America. *The Bancroft Library, University of California, Berkeley.*

fellow actors, while Barrett succeeded as a nerdier student of acting technique. Both McCullough and Barrett, as well as many others, came from Irish backgrounds. All of the Irish actors onstage became heroes and role models for the Irish immigrant. Over time, playwrights crafted Irish characters as human, sympathetic people stuck in weighty problems. These characters countered negative stereotypes that came with the Irish immigrant status.

Lawrence Barrett excelled in tragedy but brought melodrama to the masses as an actor willing to tackle roles that were overlooked by others, and he became one of the most frequently observed actors on Western stages during the last half of the nineteenth century. In later years, the *Carson City Appeal* recalled that Lawrence Barrett would check the underpinnings of the theater from the E Street side before a performance. John Piper accompanied him when, at one juncture, Barrett asked, "I say John," he said while tapping a rotten upright with his cane, "do you really think I can play Richard over that piece?" John replied, "I guarantee it holds. If it goes I give you ten percent more."

In 1868, after *Hamlet*, Barrett continued with *Macbeth*, *Richard III*, *Money*, *Lady of Lyons* and *Rosedale or the Rifle Ball.* Absent from the mining town for a year, John McCullough returned during the middle of Barrett's run to impersonate Othello opposite Barrett's Iago, with a Desdemona by Rosa Rand and an increase in dress circle prices—where the respectable sat—to $1.50. Both McCullough and Barrett had previously played the opposite roles, but McCullough was considered the better Othello, while Barrett more believably brought the sinister, manipulative Iago to reality. One critic found McCullough's Hamlet to be intelligent, while Barrett portrayed an intellectual Hamlet. The comment clarifies the differences as well as the abilities of the two actors, who both became among the most respected in the country during the late 1800s. Appreciative audiences in the West influenced their rise to stardom. Shakespearean roles were especially important for actors to properly execute because of their popularity. The most popular shows in San Francisco were *Hamlet*, *Othello*, *Macbeth* and

Romeo and Juliet, and they accounted for half of all dramatic productions there during the 1860s.

Actress Rosa Rand. *Author's collection.*

Barrett's supporting company—stock actors who took lesser roles—included two fine actresses, sisters Rosa and Olivia Rand. Rosa trained at Piper's, joined Mrs. Bowers' shows in San Francisco and proceeded to the East Coast in late 1869, where she enjoyed an important New York City run. Olivia worked for Tom Maguire's San Francisco Opera House as a soubrette for one year. Rosa became the leading lady of the Albany, New York Trimble Theater for the 1870–71 season, developing her talent in emotional drama, as both Rosa and her sister Olivia traded their Western experience for national success. They frequently acted together during the 1870s. Olivia became a stock company actress at the Boston Theater from 1873 to 1878. In 1875, Rosa supported Lawrence Barrett at Edwin Booth's New York theater. Rosa's fifty years on American stages found her perfecting Eleanor for Frank Mayo's *Davy Crockett* and she also toured with Joseph Jefferson, best known for *Rip Van Winkle*, during the 1880s. Still performing in 1897, she was classified as a "reliable" actor by an Eastern paper. Frank Mayo and Rosa opened on November 5, 1874, at Piper's Opera House in *Davy Crockett*, then on tour.

In 1869, McCullough and the mercurial Lawrence Barrett were offered their own San Francisco theater, the California, financed by William Ralston of the Bank of California. The California Theater would supply talented actors in touring combinations to Piper's Opera House for the remainder of its existence. The consistent need for talent to fill the stage and the need of stock actors to practice leading roles created a reciprocity between Virginia City—as something of a dress rehearsal—and the larger legitimate San Francisco theaters. San Francisco, in turn, supplied New York with seasoned actors. The California Theater opened on January 18, 1869, under the management of Barrett and McCullough, although Barrett soon left the partnership to McCullough. A significant theater for its size and prominence, the California Theater realized a full house of 2,479 for its opening night. The building cost $1.5 million, and cleared $100,000 in its first year of operation, becoming the West's most important theater of the mid-1800s, eventually breaking Tom Maguire's hold on the San Francisco theater business.

The theater business—somewhat unreliable in the face of competition—demanded innovation in strategies to appease an audience base of often immigrant, single male miners. Aside from the nightly change in programming, the presence of single working women turned the theater into a place of assignation. During engagements of highly respectable drama, the number of available boxes was reduced and working women were discouraged from attending. But during minstrelsy and other variety shows, pretty waiter girls worked the boxes, keeping the occupants supplied with alcohol and cigars—and a rowdy atmosphere ensued.

The year 1868 saw the solidification of Piper's business strategies, with programming heavily weighted in favor of minstrelsy. This was the most brilliant theatrical season ever witnessed in Virginia City, as opined by the *Enterprise* after Lawrence Barrett and John McCullough appeared in the classics. Artists from California who charmed Nevada audiences in 1868 included opera singer Euphrosine Parepa-Rosa, the Webb sisters, Mrs. D.P. Bowers, Charles Wheatleigh in two runs, Irish singer John Collins, Walter Couldock, Smith's California Minstrels, Willie Edouin, Ella La Rue and Mark Twain on a Western speaking tour, with Sallie Hinckley, Sue Robinson and John Howson, among others, in support. Trying to please everyone on the Comstock, the Pipers created a strategy of legitimate dramatic theater on two nights and more low-brow minstrelsy on the weekends and during the mid-week, with his stock company of players performing during both.

Sue Robinson was the first to star at Piper's Opera House after its purchase by the Pipers in March 1867, and she became their leading lady in 1868. A child performer in the California Gold Rush, Sue Robinson came to Virginia City in January 1867 to make it her home. She first appeared with the amateur locals who had formed in 1866 as a counter to the melodeon fare offered under Tom Maguire's management. As an adult, Sue distinguished herself as an instant hit, a protean star who sang, danced and played the banjo much in the style of the more famous Lotta Crabtree. Early in 1868, Sue Robinson played numerous roles as Piper's leading lady, creating Ophelia in *Hamlet.* One melodrama required her to quickly change clothes for several different characters, a popular gimmicky technique. She

Actress Sue Robinson served as a leading lady at Piper's Opera House in 1868. *Nevada Historical Society, Reno NV; BIO-R-00053.*

ran offstage during an earthquake but returned to finish her show, earning a positive comment about her strength.

Sue's early childhood of performing with the Robinson family found her "playing her way west" at six years old to remain there for the rest of her life. Both of her parents and at least two siblings created theatricalities of music, comic skits and dance routines for California Forty-Niners. By the time she attained eight years of age, Sue was receiving the highest praise of the family troupe, and she carefully retrieved every coin thrown on stage by the miners as payment for her talent. Her childhood of constant touring and travel through the Mother Lode communities of California found her hugging a tree for security during a windstorm and suffering from severe burns when she danced too close to the footlights on a Grass Valley stage. The family performed on a giant tree stump when a theater couldn't be found, and once, in an overloaded building, the floor started to give way underneath the weight of a huge audience.

Sue was a consummate talent, equally adept at dancing, singing and acting. As a child, with her brother Billy, she performed a double hornpipe, a type of clog dance. The Irish brought the hornpipe—a dance in which the performer looks left and right with a hand up to their eyes as if they are a sailor looking out over the ocean—and clogging to America. She performed the Spider Dance, made famous by Lola Montez, who supposedly taught Sue the dance, mixed in with Spanish dances with castanets, the Irish jig, the Highland fling and other cavorting. Equally adept at burlesque or tragedy, she dazzled audiences with her brilliant interpretations of women as well as men on the stage.

Sue fell in love as a teenager, but with her beloved lost in a tragic shipwreck, she married a man several years her elder while on the rebound. Her husband was insecure and jealous of her notoriety and abilities. He eventually hit her, and she obtained a divorce that split the custody of her two sons; one lived with her, and the other with her ex-husband. It was a heartbreaking solution for Sue.

As the leading lady at Piper's Opera House, Sue supported the greatest actors who ventured to the mining town, including Barrett, McCullough, Mayo and Joe Murphy, in comedy sketches, variety shows, melodramas and Shakespearean plays. She also worked with Joseph Proctor from Sacramento's Metropolitan Theater, who specialized in a play called *Nick of the Woods.* The *Gold Hill News*, in 1868, described her acting: "She was as usual very successful, and the applause bestowed indicates the strong hold she always has and always will have as prime favorite with her audiences here, where she is best known."

Actress Jennie Worrell was presented with honorary membership in a local firefighting group. In this photograph, she proudly wears the belt with number four's insignia. *Jennie Worrell, circa 1863, UNRS-P1347_1, box: 19. Alfred Doten Papers, NC08; University of Nevada, Reno; Special Collections Department.*

Favorite actresses and women who had done something special for the firefighters were rewarded with an honorary membership in the volunteer firefighter's associations. Membership in the company and a silver and gold fire belt were Sue's rewards. Banjoist Charley Rhoades wrote song lyrics for "Our Engine on the Hill," which Sue sang. The lyrics included:

But we'll drink to the boys, whom no danger annoys
To the laddies who never knew fear—
And when the "Hall" strikes the alarm
With our steam whistle screaming out shrill
A space we'll soon clear, for they'll know we are near
With our engine that housed on the hill.

More legitimate theater was offered in 1868 with Charles Wheatleigh and Annie Firman opening with the five-act comedy *Sam.* Annie Firman, whom

Actor Charles Wheatleigh, costumed as the Shaughraun, the wanderer, in a play by the same name. *Author's collection.*

the *Trespass* felt should have been hissed by the audience for a poor opening-night rendition of her part, valiantly acted in the West for many years. She made her San Francisco acting debut only four months before her Virginia City engagement. Four nights of *Sam* met audiences "literally crammed" into the Opera House with a rise in the price of box seating. Annie Firman returned to Piper's in 1875 and was a member of the supporting company when the Great Fire destroyed the theater.

Charles Wheatleigh followed in James Stark's footsteps with California audiences of the 1850s. He leased the San Francisco Eureka Theater for several years and opened the Metropolitan Theater there with *Arrah-Na-Pogue*. Considered second only to John McCullough and Lawrence Barrett in prominence in the West, Wheatleigh was one of the most successful regional actors of the time. Credited with versatility, compassionate impersonations and restraint, he adapted to change as a resourceful actor, by embracing the newer techniques of natural and realistic acting. His early theatrical appearances included Philadelphia's Walnut Street Theater, and late in life, he assumed old gentlemen roles in a thirty-year career. Wheatleigh's excellent characterizations complemented Irish-themed plays, the mainstay of his offerings in the 1860s. Wheatleigh attained an incredible run of fifty nights in *Arrah-Na-Pogue* in San Francisco. *Arrah-Na-Pogue* dramatized Irish resistance to British rule and had a special appeal to Irish audiences. Its title means "Arrah of the kiss," and its heroine, Arrah, passes instructions to the imprisoned rebel leader through a kiss, a technique that would later be captured by Houdini when his wife passed the key to his straitjacket to him with a kiss. By 1877, Wheatleigh "ceased to be obtrusively Hibernian," according to the *Daily Alta California*, a comment that reflects on the actor's ability to act in plays that spoke to the Irish immigrant experience during the 1860s, and also, his ability to change as the Irish became American over time.

Wheatleigh reveled in two long runs—the same play offered on successive nights—in 1868. First appearing in March, he opened with *Sam* and then *Arrah-Na-Pogue* and *Octoroon* for three nights. *Octoroon* first opened in 1859 as an antislavery piece that showcased elaborate sets, including a burning steamship on the Mississippi. An "octoroon," a term coined by author Dion Boucicault, described a person who was one-eighth Black. One of Boucicault's greatest hits, the play seized on a precise period in America. Zoe, the illegitimate daughter of an enslaved woman and a plantation owner, is treated as almost white, but laws against miscegenation prohibit her marriage to a white man. The play deals with the challenges and inconsistencies of society and law, as well as class and race issues. Lacking in propaganda, part of the play's popularity and strength lies in its portrayal of the situation of slavery; the tragedy of human suffering by a woman in love with one man while facing her condition as the property of another man. *Octoroon* is filled with high drama, chills, fears and special effects. Audiences loved the sensation of witnessing a shipwreck and burning steamship on the Mississippi River.

Wheatleigh followed with *Colleen Bawn*, a heartwarming Irish story. Wheatleigh had played in the original New York cast and then perfected his leading role for audiences around the world. He then performed *Sam*, *Lottery of Life* for five nights and *Under the Gaslight*, which was destined to become one of the most popular melodramas in Virginia City for many years.

Lottery of Life is an antisemitic thriller set in New York City that centers on Jewish merchant Mordie Solomons, an "elaborate villain, a fence, moneylender, counterfeiter, and blackmailer," according to the play's stage directions. The stage costume for Mordie, "long shabby coat, dirty silk handkerchief tied round his head, old slippers, long beard, and false Jewish nose with glasses, dark trousers worn all through," perpetuated negative stereotypes. Speaking with a "strong Jewish accent," Mordie counts his receipts in a caricature of Jewish thriftiness, which finds him stymied by the end of a complicated plot. Victorian theatergoers were fascinated by people who were different. Plays reflected that fascination with caricatures and stereotypes, while these stereotypes added to antisemitic and racist beliefs.

Popular *Under the Gaslight* features an oft-repeated trope: the leading man is tied to a railroad track, and the leading lady saves his life before the train can cut him in two. Love follows. At the Opera House, *Under the Gaslight* ran successfully for eight nights, the longest run of an individual play to date, with a supporting company well versed in their parts. Wheatleigh's second 1868 engagement found him reusing his earlier successes and adding *Flying Scud*, another antisemitic play, this one about horseracing. Virginia City audiences saw *Flying Scud*, written in 1866, within a year of its premiere in San Francisco. Miniature horses, seen in the distance, passed and re-passed until, finally, a real horse and rider were brought out on the stage. One newspaper said it was "too horsey" for Virginia City audiences when it failed to attract large crowds. Wheatleigh's successes prompted John Piper to journey to San Francisco to search for other dramatic actors.

The Webb sisters, Ada and Emma, fresh on the heels of a poor run in Marysville, California, also failed to attract crowds at Piper's. Significant competition from the Gold Hill Theater and political gatherings found

Left: Ada Webb, who performed only once in Virginia City, added to the town's reputation for difficult audiences. *Author's collection.*

Right: Mark Twain, Virginia City's most famous early resident, in the 1870s. *Courtesy of Joe Curtis, Virginia City, NV.*

the Creole sisters from New Orleans drawing audiences so small that the actors were spiritless. They relinquished the Opera House to Virginia City's favorite former resident: Mark Twain.

Mark Twain lived in Virginia City just short of two years during the early 1860s while he worked as a newspaper reporter for the *Territorial Enterprise*. Lecture tours were common in the 1800s, as lecturing in theaters crossed the line into entertainment. Twain had lectured previously in 1866, but a somewhat unrealized treat was in store for Comstockers when Twain spoke for a dollar a seat admission on Monday and Tuesday, April 27 and 28, 1868, during his last trip to the Comstock. As expected, Twain's "Pilgrim Life," an account of his famous trip to the Holy Land that would be the basis for his book *Innocents Abroad*, met with good audiences and praise as reported by the local newspapers. But an interesting backstory to their reviews emerged.

Twain drank champagne with assorted newspapermen, including Joe Goodman of the *Enterprise* and Philip Lynch and Alf Doten of the *Gold*

Jaunty newspaperman Alf Doten in his volunteer fireman clothes for the Fourth of July, 1867. *Special Collections Photographs, UNRS-P0189-2.tif collection_6445, Special Collections and University Archive Department, University of Nevada, Reno.*

Hill News. Twain gave free tickets to Doten. Twain also appeared on the *Daily Trespass*'s doorstep to hobnob with the editor William J. Forbes. Twain understood the importance of good reviews in the local papers, and they did report the best impression of the lectures as if they drew extremely crowded houses each night. However, Alf Doten's journal entries belie that evidence. Doten, more likely to report the truth in his journal, recorded that it was a "not very full house," although the "lecture [was] humorous, very, as well as pleasing and instructive." The same lecture the second night met with "about same audience as last night." Competition for the lecture appeared in the form of a ball and dances at two local halls. In a letter to a California paper, Twain commented that he had paid the management of the Virginia City theater $450 for the privilege of lecturing in their "miserable old barn.... It was an act of Christian charity to pay it, however, as they hadn't made enough to pay their gas bills for the previous six weeks. I love to go about doing good work." Although Twain and his silver brick gift were heralded as "Washoe produce," Twain never returned; likewise, neither did the Webb Sisters or the Couldocks.

Returning melodeon performers from Carson City followed Mark Twain with reduced admission rates, four bits to any part of the house. But the Pipers had visions of legitimate drama for May 1868, and they brought in nationally known Charles Walter Couldock and his daughter Eliza. British-born Couldock opened in a serious drama, *The Willow Copse* (thicket), his signature piece enacted in many American theaters during his long career. Although the supporting players needed improvement, Piper's enjoyed full attendance, and the stars took two curtain calls on opening night. As typical of other engagements, as the run continued, the attendance decreased. Later shows brought good audiences out to see the minstrel show travesty afterpiece of *Under the Gaspipe*, with the comedy of a minstrel man as Laura, reviewed as "the funniest thing out." Local people turned out for several benefits, and one night found Sue Robinson in a fireman's hat and red shirt singing "Who Wouldn't Want to be a Fireman's Darling" with the Couldocks and melodeon performers in song and dance routines. The audience had spoken, and even a repertoire of plays never previously performed in Nevada could not save the Couldocks from an early end to their visit.

Melodeon variety shows loosely based on minstrelsy took over the Opera House, demonstrating audience preferences and the origin of much of Piper's success. Business was so good for the Piper brothers that John and Henry looked at the possibility of opening a saloon and theater in Reno, where they owned property, and shortly after, his stock company presented

Pictured here are Walter and his daughter Eliza Couldock in a scene from the popular 1880s play *Hazel Kirke*. *Author's collection.*

entertainment in a storefront there. John had purchased property in Reno with the first land sale, as locals anticipated a day in the not-too-distant future, when a train across the continent would make Reno important. The "densely crowded audiences" at Piper's found a drop in ticket prices; the presence of waiter girls, liquor and cigars; and the return of box seating priced at $2.50, $3, and $5. The variety players appeared in unusual roles, with one on a flying trapeze, which ran from the dress circle to the back of the stage. Entertainment based on scantily-clad women prevailed, as the afterpiece *Three Fast Women* gave a large amount of "shape." Returning funnyman Harry Leslie provided humorous political stump speeches. Joe Murphy and a varied cast of "Ethiopian comedians"—another name for minstrel performers—burlesqued *Under the Gaslight*, with Irish characters in the roles usually cast as Black people.

Joe Murphy had been a champion bones-playing end man in minstrelsy since the mid-1850s with several groups in California, appearing at Piper's from 1867 to 1870 and then returning in 1874. He broke from minstrelsy in the early 1870s to play in Irish-themed plays. Complexity and humanity in Irish portrayals became common in the 1870s as the immigrant Irish population gave way to second-generation Irish Americans, and Joe Murphy's switch from minstrelsy to comedy plays added to this trend. The *Enterprise* critic heaped encomiums on Joe Murphy's characterizations. Joe Murphy broke attendance records with over 750 people jammed into the parquette alone. "Have a good hearty laugh for once. Joe is the great and only Murphy," opined the *Enterprise.*

"The Prince of Minstrelsy," Joe Murphy left the West Coast for New York in 1871. There, he first presented *Help*, essentially a one-man show. Written by Murphy, *Help* allowed him to use his talent to caricature other races and nationalities. By 1878, Murphy had returned to the West Coast in *Kerry Cow*, which features a quiet and unassuming blacksmith in an Irish setting.

Often called the "Queen of the American Stage," Mrs. D.P. Bowers was one of the best examples of a national star to play in 1868, and her engagement lasted almost one month. Mrs. Bowers had a large repertoire of female roles, although she frequently impersonated queens. Often considered an actress second only to Charlotte Cushman, Mrs. Bowers had played Juliet to Cushman's Romeo on Broadway in 1860. Mrs. Bower's suffered from role entrapment with her signature play, *Lady Audley's Secret.* The play was a spectacular experience filled with suspense, as a burning home onstage was facilitated by gas fittings on collapsible wooden framework; staging that has certainly passed out of use now due to safety concerns. Although Mrs.

Left: *Help* was Joe Murphy's signature vehicle, which allowed him to present several different characters as he moved from minstrelsy to serious acting. *Billy Rose Theatre Division, New York Public Library*.

Right: Mrs. D.P. "Elizabeth" Bowers, born in 1830 in Connecticut, toured continuously. *Author's collection*.

Bowers may not have met with enthusiastic audiences for all of her many and varied roles at Piper's in 1868, she returned to Piper's in 1873, 1875 and 1888, her last West Coast visit. In 1888, she presented *Lady Audley's Secret*, which had, by then, been offered thousands of times by her, along with older plays like *Lucretia Borgia* and *Queen Elizabeth*. The theater provided actresses with a rare potential at independence and power over their lives, even while they enforced stereotypes of women's societal roles. Mrs. Bowers led a non-traditional life by managing her own traveling ensemble, usually with only one other person, her lover James McCollum. Her own life countered the usual stereotypes of woman's dependency on a man for success, while her roles onstage promoted woman's traditional values and domesticity.

After a short break, the California Minstrels from San Francisco returned the Opera House to melodeon fare for two weeks. Minstrel groups were

Unidentified minstrels in blackface from a stereopticon photograph of the 1890s. *Author's collection.*

formed as early as 1849 in California, with Tom Maguire credited for creating the best in minstrelsy. The *Enterprise*'s review noted Alfred Bamford's "highly cultivated" falsetto voice filling the theater with "I Miss Thee, My Darling," probably while dressed in blackface as a prima donna for comic effect. The boys on the street were whistling show tunes the next day. The "Funny Old Gal," played by a burley comedian clad in tawdry, mismatched clothes and large shoes, counterbalanced the stock female minstrel character of the dainty prima donna. Men portraying females exaggerated negative female qualities, keeping women marginalized through stereotypes, and blackface portrayals minimized the contributions and accomplishments of Black Americans.

Pianist Louis Gottshalk. *Internet Archive.*

Another minstrel star, Johnny DeAngelis, enjoyed a good West Coast reputation, appearing in Virginia City in the 1860s and in 1870. He had been part of Maguire's original San Francisco Minstrels, performing in California since the Gold Rush. Johnny's more famous son Jefferson De Angelis described living a very tough hand-to-mouth existence as a child performer while touring the American West with his parents. Minstrel shows featured performers on centerstage in a semicircle singing foolish or nonsense lyrics. The "end man" stood at the end of the semicircle of performers. Johnny, as the end man, usually played the tambourine, told jokes and bantered with the interlocutor, or the straight man. The interlocutor received the brunt of the jokes, a put-down of class-based societal divisions. Then performers took their turns with a strut or cakewalk around the circle to perform their own particular style of dancing, singing or performing on a musical instrument, often the popular banjo. A short intermission allowed the cast to change and prepare for a closing comedy skit.

Minstrel star Charley Rhoades, who visited the mining town several times, as well as other banjo players, inspired Mark Twain to compare a banjoist with pianist Louis Gottschalk, who played the Comstock in 1865. Gottschalk got as much out of the piano "as there is in it," but for Twain, "give me the banjo." He continued in the *San Francisco Dramatic Chronicle* of June 23, 1865:

> *Gottschalk, when compared to Sam Pride or Charley Rhoades, is a Dashaway cocktail to a hot whiskey punch. When you want genuine music, music that will come right home to you like a bad quarter, suffuse your system like strychnine whiskey, go right through you like Brandreth's pills, ramify your whole constitution like the measles, and break out on your hide like the pin feather pimples on a picked goose—when you want all this, just smash your piano and invoke the glory—beaming banjo!*

Next came a troupe of Japanese jugglers, acrobats and necromancers. Their seven-day run found the Comstock's fashionable in the dress circle and Chinese, Black and Paiute patrons in the parquette, creating diversity and packed houses. The diversity of the American West was reflected by the audience; members of these groups even became amateur supporting performers if needed.

Comedian Willie Edouin, who would later appear as a stock player at the California Theater, leased Piper's Opera House in October 1868 for his performances of pantomimes interspersed with ballads, dances and burlesques. Edouin's greatest artistic success came with his work in support of Lydia Thompson's British Blondes burlesque troupe in the late 1870s. He performed in blackface as Friday to Lydia's Robinson Crusoe. He frequently characterized Chinese men, as well as individuals from other minority populations. He was not alone in this, as the stereotypes of immigrants and non-white races came from a long theatrical tradition of making fun of "others" at their expense. The repeated performances of negative stereotypes may have made the belief in these negative characteristics stronger. The year 1868 ended with the appearance of the multitalented Ella LaRue, who walked a tightrope, sang, danced, acted and played the banjo.

The Gold Hill Theater created the strongest competition for Piper's Opera House. This threat prompted John Piper to purchase the theater in November 1868. Piper had been losing his audiences of Gold Hill miners, as they often preferred their hometown theater. About one-third of the Opera House's audience members lived in Gold Hill. During

Above: Willie Edouin in costume. *Author's collection.*

Opposite: Alf Doten's diary documents his crush on Ella La Rue, and a noticeable erasure may mean that a tryst between the two was erased. *Special Collections Photographs, UNRS-P1305-1.tif collection_3727, Special Collections and University Archive Collections, University of Nevada, Reno.*

the boom year of 1868, the Piper brothers established several components needed for success: talented performers, new and timely theatrical material, a philosophy of giving the people what they wanted and the ability to make life difficult for the competition or purchase it outright. Buying the competition—saloon theater melodeons primarily devoted to minstrelsy and variety—meant limiting options for the theatergoing public. Diverse entertainment attempted to satisfy all tastes in theatricalities to ensure a wider audience base. As plays changed nightly and legitimate theatrical engagements were interspersed with variety performances, audiences could anticipate something different every night of the week. A good stock company of backup actors attracted star celebrities, and they also mounted productions based on a large repertoire of contemporary melodramas and recognized classics. This flexibility created a rich, dynamic theater.

6

THE DEPRESSION YEARS BEGIN

SHAPE, SPECTACLE, SENSATION

To-night more shape and twice the usual dose of fun.
—opined the Territorial Enterprise

Although 1869 started out well, economic recession hit mid-year after the completion of the transcontinental railroad. Borrasca, Spanish for "stormy weather," found much of the mining population leaving for new discoveries in Nevada's White Pine County. A depression in mine production, declining mining stocks and strikes in other areas all meant longer gaps between Opera House performers. Attempted long runs saw fewer returning theatergoers, as they tired of the attractions or found their income didn't stretch far enough for theater visits. The supporting cast of players created continuous problems throughout the year until they were disbanded mid-year and the Opera House turned to variety, minstrelsy and lectures offered by touring interests. Any local depression or recession saw more downtime, as variety and other self-contained shows increased, along with other strategies that included closing the theater completely. Variety shows, or presentations that did not rely on a written play, increased during hard times.

To maximize their engagements, players found appreciative audiences in Reno, Carson City, Dayton and some of the other nearby settlements. Matinees and "ladies' nights" for women and families offered a more sanitized version of the minstrel shows. After May 15, dogs were strictly forbidden to accompany their masters to Opera House productions. The theater owners again reminded the "peanut cannibals" to stop smoking in the theater in continuing attempts to cater to more respectable audiences. The parquette, which offered cheap seats for "screaming and whistling young rascals," was located at the area closest to the stage, observed the *Gold Hill News*.

The highlights of 1869 included Lucille Western, James A. Herne, Annette Ince, John E. Owens, John McCullough and Charlotte Thompson with the supporting cast of the California Theater. The legendary James Stark fulfilled his last starring engagement at Piper's, as a stroke he suffered while on stage portraying *Hamlet* threatened his life.

Legitimate drama brought the famous and talented to the mining town in mid-January. Two stars of national fame, Lucille Western and James A. Herne, opened for a three-week run as part of a West Coast tour. Lucille was the older, more emotional sister of Helen Western, who was James A. Herne's first wife. Theirs was the most tragic romance of the American stage, as James fell in love with Helen's sister Lucille and later sought a divorce from Helen. Rumors flew about the affair, but they had no negative effect on box office receipts. Lucille purchased the play *East Lynne*, destined to become her signature drama. She portrayed the repentant heroine for over one thousand performances. Noted for her sensational stage falls, Western opened with Herne at Maguire's San Francisco Opera House on April 30, 1867, in their first West Coast tour. At their return to San Francisco in late 1868, Herne appeared at one of Maguire's theaters, while Western starred at another. In Virginia City, they appeared together. Nevada's audiences, which were less judgmental, enjoyed both stars' professional abilities without regard for their private lives, an inclination that occurred with other stars.

Actor James A. Herne, the child of poor Irish immigrants, became a prominent playwright after a significant stage career. Herne attempted the role of Rip Van Winkle, with the Piper's company taking supporting roles. Among them was a minstrel comic, Otto Burbank, who stole the show, appearing on stage to a huge round of applause—more applause than either James Herne or Lucille Western. "Otto is the greatest favorite of any on the stage," opined Alf Doten in his diary.

Herne's costar and lover, the beautiful Lucille Western, may have been the actress's actress. Fellow thespian Clara Morris described Lucille in her autobiography: "She was a born actress....In all she did there was a touch of extravagance—a hint of lawless, unrestrained passion. There was something tropical about her, she always suggested the scarlet tanager, the jeweled dragon-fly, the pomegranate flower, or the scentless splendor of our wild marshmallow." Lucille became a major nationwide attraction by portraying

Lucille Western, costumed as Lucretia Borgia, one of her key roles. *Author's collection.*

strong, emotional women. Known as the "Pearl of the American Stage," Lucille amplified her own mystery by her practice of wearing a shoulder-length black veil in public while on tour.

Mark Twain once commented that *East Lynne* was the "sickest of all sentimental dramas" and that water privileges would be cheap in Virginia City the week after *East Lynne* played there in 1863 if those audiences "whine, snuffle and slobber all over themselves" as they had in San Francisco. *East Lynne* would be repeated at Piper's Opera House from 1871 through 1889, with many other actresses attempting the role of the repentant woman who follows her heart and loses her husband and children to another. Lucille

Western's benefit night portrayal of Leah in *Leah, the Forsaken* received hearty appreciation, with the star called before the curtain by applause after each of the last two acts. *Leah, the Forsaken* became a popular play in Virginia City that was repeated in 1871, 1873, 1874 and 1875 in various versions. Set in Germany, the story line focuses on a Jewish woman who falls in love with a Christian man. The man marries another, after he is falsely persuaded of Leah's desertion. Leah's death creates a tear-filled finale as her former lover realizes his mistake.

The problems of snowstorms, a lack of rehearsal time, the need for a prompter and the use of older plays all contributed to the analysis of good actors meeting lackluster success. Later complaints concerned the length of time between acts. Because the drop curtain was down for nearly half an hour between acts, there were backstage technical problems as well.

Annette Ince, the daughter of a Baltimore theater manager, became a critically important actress to John Piper's theater, as both a supporting cast member and leading lady. She started her career as a dancer in 1849. Coming to California soon after the Gold Rush, she became an important player there, eventually graduating to theater management in the 1860s. She appeared at Maguire's Virginia City Opera House in November 1863. Ince joined John McCullough and Lawrence Barrett at their new California Theater on its opening in January 1869 as the leading lady, but she would play there only intermittently after the first year. She would star in a short engagement at Piper's in 1871. In 1874, Piper created a "Grand Star Dramatic Alliance" to support Annette Ince in Stockton for three shows and Marysville, California for one week, with a quick return to Piper's. Noteworthy among the supporting cast in 1874 was a talented, painstakingly professional actress, Annie Adams, the mother of actress Maude Adams. Miss Ince impersonated her signature role of Julia in *The Hunchback* on the second night of the 1874 run, with the *Gold Hill News* putting her in the "front rank of celebrities in the mimic world." George Chaplin acted in her support. George Chaplin, a California Theater supporting actor stole the show in *Foul Play*, in which he took three roles. The two-hour-and-twenty-minute play included stage effects: wind, rain, thunder, breaking glass, falling buildings, snow, water, waves, cascades, passing trains, lightning, chimes, the sound of horses hooves and shots—the typical spectacle.

Annette Ince brought a national premiere of *Cloud and Sunshine* to Piper's Opera House in 1874. It was an almost unheard-of attempt to position the theater on a higher level of professionalism than the more frequently used minstrelsy and variety shows. Miss Ince was presented with a bouquet

Above: Annette Ince, the first leading lady at San Francisco's California Theater, performed at Piper's for many years in starring and supporting roles, enjoying a long career on the West Coast. *Billy Rose Theatre Division, New York Public Library*.

Opposite: George Chaplin, a California Theater supporting actor who took leading roles in Virginia City, and became Piper's stage manager in 1875. *The Bancroft Library, University of California Berkeley*.

of flowers in appreciation of her endeavor "to raise the drama in its moral purity" to encourage women to safely attend the theater, as the local newspaper believed. Despite praiseworthy attempts on stage, Annette Ince "lacked that inexplicable something which raises simple success to triumph," opined the *Enterprise* for her 1874 engagement. Annette Ince continued to anchor the supporting company of Piper's Opera House, but frankly, she was at the end of her career, which had peaked in California in 1859 when she took the role of Shakespeare in a play about his life.

The year 1869 also saw talented performers in an opéra bouffe, a humorous burlesque of legitimate opera. Multitalented John Howson, with his parents and siblings, made up the Howson Family English and Italian Opera. They were one of the first groups to perform opéra bouffe. John Howson had previously appeared in Virginia City in supporting roles to Mrs. D.P. Bowers, but for opéra bouffe, he dressed in female attire and sang in falsetto. Theater historians have argued that the best female impersonators of the 1800s were attracted to other men, and their talent reflected upon the conflicted realities of homosexuality inherent during that period. John Howson appeared in the cast of the Oates Opéra Bouffe, which played Piper's in 1875. A consummate performer, he was called before the curtain for special acclaim at the end of the run.

Tom Thumb appeared at Piper's Opera House in 1869 while on a cross-country tour. By parading the streets of Virginia City prior to showtime, the stars drew in crowds amazed by their size. Shows had to be repeated due to audience demand. The performers, General Tom Thumb with his wife, Lavinia, her sister Minnie and Commodore Nutt, performed songs, dances and skits. Groomed and aggrandized by P.T. Barnum starting in 1862, they enjoyed lifelong careers in show business.

The lack of theatrical expertise on the part of manager John Piper was highlighted in the memories of national celebrity John E. Owens, who also visited the mining town in 1869. He deprecated the provincial nature of the attraction, as well as amateur actors in the supporting cast.

John McCullough made two engagements during 1869, the last one at the end of the year supporting Charlotte Thompson. The end of the

Left: Versatile performer John Howson with a violin; he also sang, danced and impersonated women in comic opera. *Author's collection.*

Opposite: Tom Thumb, with his wife, Lavinia, toured the West in 1869. *Author's collection.*

theatrical season in San Francisco created a bonus in programming for the mining town, as the California Theater stars opened on December 3 with their outstanding supporting company and their own scenic designer. New scenery had been painted, and the lower boxes at the end of the parquette were removed as testimony to the power of respectable attendees over the demimonde. The beautiful Charlotte Thompson earned top billing over favorite John McCullough and supporting actors John T. Raymond and his wife, Marie Gordon. "Genial" John McCullough enjoyed a twenty-seven-year nationally acclaimed career in which he specialized in playing heroes. With a rags-to-riches backstory, McCullough immigrated to the United States at the age of fifteen from Northern Ireland. He could not read when he came, but through years of diligent work and study, he rose within his chosen profession, a role model to other Irish immigrants. McCullough's personifications were consistently met with praise. According to Hutton in *Curiosities of the American Stage*, McCullough appeared "free from mannerisms,

his figure was manly and striking, he was neither too puny nor too burly, his sentiment was not mawkish, nor was his honesty brutal." McCullough's finest acting reflected his character of simplicity, modesty and manliness.

John T. Raymond, the low comedian of the San Francisco California Theater, came to Virginia City to star in several productions. He took leading roles he would not have been able to execute in the Bay City. In March 1874, Raymond with his wife, Marie Gordon, returned for a one-week run to start their comedic opening in *Dot, or Cricket on the Hearth* and

Left: John McCullough. *Author's collection.*

Right: John T. Raymond practiced his craft as a low comedian in the California Theater stock company and then took starring roles in Virginia City, eventually becoming a national celebrity. *Author's collection.*

Toodles, the afterpiece. Piper's had helped develop the talented Raymond through his many appearances in the mining town in 1869, 1870, 1871 and 1874, before he went on to national fame. "There's millions in it," was the catch phrase from Colonel Sellers in *The Gilded Age*, a play based on Mark Twain's opus of the same title, which became Raymond's most famous nationally known role. Like those of other actors, Raymond's personal life contained painful experiences. Marie Gordon married and divorced fellow actor John T. Raymond, whose successes in celebrated national theaters far surpassed her own.

Twenty-six-year-old Charlotte Thompson's *Camille* won raves from the *Gold Hill News*, which said her performance surpassed even that of Mrs. D.P. Bowers. Born to a theatrical family in England, Charlotte came to the United States as a child and began performing in her teens. When the California Theater opened on January 18, 1869, Charlotte was the first female East Coast star to appear there, headlining for forty-four nights. Perfecting her role in *Sea of Ice*, Charlotte succeeded, with many special effects created by the unseen theater personnel. The backstage business in the Victorian theater

Left: Actress Marie Gordon. From the stock company of the California Theater, Marie rose in casting and execution at Piper's Opera House. *Author's collection.*

Right: Actress Charlotte Thompson. *Author's collection.*

was almost as important as the cast to theater manager David Belasco, who believed that the most powerful emotional appeal could be made using color and light on the stage.

The California Theater's scenic designer remained to paint the allegorical scene "The Voyage of Life" on the stage drop curtain. Newspapers noted that he had made the drop curtain a new attraction deserving of merit on its own, considering the amount of time it was down before the audience. In 1869, the *Territorial Enterprise* joked that the night watchman held forth on Piper's stage in the silence of an empty theater. Soon, he would be sleeping as his way of practicing for Rip Van Winkle.

November 1869 marked the completion of the Virginia & Truckee Railroad, with tracks reaching Virginia City. The line anticipated the upcoming boom years in the 1870s, when it would help John Piper to bring troupes to Carson, Reno and the surrounding region. The *Gold Hill News* mentioned which performers had come from the East by rail.

During the depression years, which lasted from mid-1869 until early 1874, most of the best "family" entertainment came from traveling variety

Pictured is one of the Zavistowski sisters. *Author's collection.*

performers. Variety shows included minstrelsy, magicians, ventriloquists, singers, musicians, gymnasts, talented children, dancers and lots of gimmicky, quirky performances. Violinist Camilla Urso, who represented the height of Victorian respectability, made a two-night run in 1870. Born in France to a musical family, Urso came to America as a child in 1852 and made her first Western tour in 1868. Her popularity came from being known in places great performers rarely visited. Variety performers consistently filled in the gaps between troupes presenting full-length plays.

Another depression strategy included the presentation of women in salacious productions generally based on minstrelsy. Less respectable entertainment exploited women as spectacle, such as that offered by the Zavistowski sisters. Female spectacle peaked with the can-can dance craze, which hit the Comstock in 1870, and appeared in many forms in musical shows under enchanting names like the "Zephyr Dance," presumably with lots of action. The Zavistowski sisters pioneered "Shoo Fly Don't Bother Me" as their way to dance the can-can and performed at Piper's during the depression years 1870 and 1872.

7

THE NOTORIOUS ALHAMBRA THEATER

The Alhambra was again filled to overflowing in every part last night, and a high old bill was given—lots of new local hits and puns. The can-can is still all the go there, and in it everything goes.
—believed the Territorial Enterprise, *March 2, 1870*

While John Piper searched San Francisco for talent, his Opera House languished from disuse, and the new Alhambra flourished. The first few months of 1870 were good enough economically, as mine production and ore processing temporarily increased, to encourage the Alhambra to open in February 1870. About one and a half blocks away from Piper's Opera House, the Alhambra took over Cheap John's saloon, which provided entry from C Street. A five-hundred-seat brick dance hall on Union Street, running between C and D Streets, was renovated to become the Alhambra Theater melodeon, Piper's nemesis. The eastern end of the building fronted D Street within the legal red-light district. Undoubtedly, the owners expected a clientele of D Street women, and from comments made by Alf Doten in his journals, they were not disappointed. Doten called one show the most "vulgar" he had ever seen, as people had pulled their clothes up over their heads. A green room and bar were located at the D Street entrance, which offered a direct, private entrance to the boxes; this was important to the working women who patronized the theater. The green room facilitated visits between audience members and performers, some of whom also may have offered sexual favors.

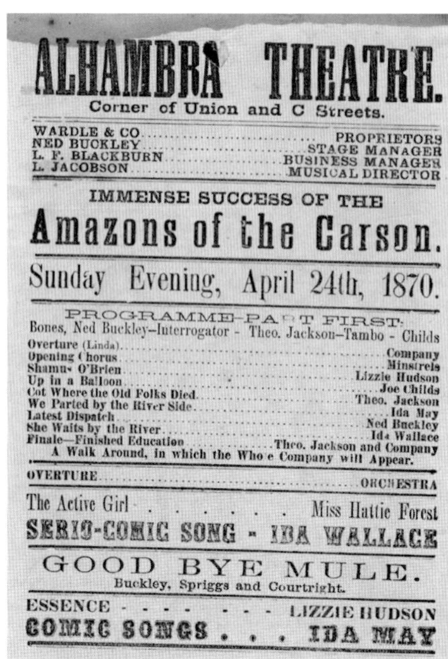

Above: Alhambra Theater advertising poster in two parts. Notice the information about a direct entrance from D street. *Special Collections, Nevada Women's Archives, Alhambra Theatre Collections, 96-23; Special Collections and University Archive Collections, University of Nevada, Reno.*

Opposite: Minstrel performer Billy Courtright is pictured here in blackface makeup. *Author's collection.*

On the theater's opening day, the *Enterprise* critic could only get to within ten feet of the door because of the enormous crowds; half of the men who wanted to enter were turned away. After a few weeks, the Alhambra advertised matinees for families and offered a special entrance on Union Street for the respectable, although the theater saloon was never designed for respectable ladies. The Alhambra was a melodeon that played heavily on the popularity of the can-can, a popular dance craze, and the allure of the female shape. With two bars and waiter girls "always in attendance to supply the wants of visitors," the theater offered some of the best minstrel performers to entertain the "boys," as the newspaper referred to the miners. The performances onstage served as a sexual stimulant to the audience members, who could then pursue a woman from D Street in one of the theater's many boxes.

The Alhambra opened with a high-end, sixteen-member melodeon cast, including M.B. Leavitt as an "Ethiopian comedian" and end man. Leavitt

became known as the "Father of American Burlesque" when he began promoting female burlesque stars in a style that he made famous during the 1880s. Leavitt became a central booking agent for many theaters that were developing a new business model, and in the late 1880s, he would supply burlesque shows to the current Piper's Opera House on B and Union Streets. Leavitt, about twenty-seven years old at the time he played the Alhambra, recalled in his autobiography that Virginia City was a booming place with "gambling houses and other sporting resorts…running wide open." At least a dozen dance halls operated early in the year. Leavitt ran the Bush Street Theater in San Francisco in the late 1880s, and while there, Leavitt and some performers were arrested for the bawdy and indecent nature of the shows. Indecency, subject to audience interpretation, prevailed with the Alhambra's female cast in the "shapely" "Shoo Fly" can-can "devoid of an overabundance of clothing," noted the *Gold Hill News*.

Billy Courtright, a minstrel performer who started in San Francisco in 1867, performed at the Alhambra in early 1870 and made the transition to silent movies in the early 1900s. His gimmick was called the flewy-flewy. He entered the stage with a suitcase and then put his foot through it and paraded around, seemingly oblivious to the problem. He appeared in numerous silent films before 1930.

Historian John Jennings believed that the ballerinas in melodeon productions needed only to be female. Some came from factory work and could be taught to walk in time to the music "and do nothing but march about" while the leading dancers performed in more of a traditional ballet fashion. But the exploitation of the female figure—called "shape"—was antithetical to Victorian standards of the time. The "walk-around," popular in Virginia City long after its disappearance from minstrel shows in other areas, served to show off the cast's women in skimpy clothing.

Contemporary playwright Clay M. Greene observed that "downright indecency was the crux and purpose of nearly all of them," referring to melodeons. Liquor reduced inhibitions; a raucous atmosphere ensued. The Alhambra advertised "slave-girl" auction skits, presumably women parading in alluring clothes, while "Red Hot or the Devil and Mt. Davidson" reflected innuendo. "Lively servants" and "pugilistic lovers" were components of other skits. The Carson Amazons, as advertised in the poster, would have been scantily dressed women whose bodies, as viewed onstage, created a sexually stimulating, zesty entertainment for men. The theater's opening skit, titled "8 Hours a Day," may reflect on the working-class clientele the theater attracted.

Jennie Lee, Billy Courtright's wife, also started in minstrel shows in the West and had a career in opéra bouffe in the early 1870s. *Author's collection.*

Piper's countered the Alhambra's opening night with legitimate drama and a ballet troupe headed by Mademoiselle Bonfanti. The twenty-nine-person Bonfanti ballet troupe, the first ballet to play the mining town, capitalized on the sensations of short-frocked dancers in flesh-colored tights. The *Territorial Enterprise* puffed Bonfanti as one of the most graceful dancers on the Pacific coast. "Our friend" John Piper was complimented on the "excellence of his company," continued the *Enterprise*. But even praise from the newspapers could not stem the tide of audiences at the Alhambra, who were intrigued with the can-can, which "gets" the "boys." "Those that find fault with it must be very near sighted," quipped the *Enterprise*.

John Piper battled with the Alhambra for audiences throughout 1870, adding women to his casts and borrowing scenes that had appeared at the Alhambra previously. He put together a fantastic cast of minstrel stars, including Johnny DeAngelis and Fanny Hanks, and then instituted

OLYMPIC

PICTORIAL

ISSUED FROM THE OLYMPIC THEATRE, CORNER OF HARVARD AND WASHINGTON STREETS, BOSTON, FOR THE WEEK ENDING AUGUST 14, 1869.

Mademoiselle Marietta Bonfanti. *Jerome Robbins Dance Division, New York Public Library.*

occasional "ladies' nights," when smoking and drinking would not be tolerated in the hopes of taking audiences away from the Alhambra. Later in the year, Piper had quite enough of the minstrel and melodeon business, according to the *Enterprise*, and was looking for something in the world of the legitimate. But this revelation came only five days before his purchase of the Alhambra. John purchased the melodeon outright in late September and then had it retrofitted to be a dance hall. The stage scenery and theatrical trappings were removed, and with the purchase, the melodeon entertainment there ended. It subsequently opened as a dance hall under the management of Dick Bermann with half a dozen girls; advertisements proclaimed the hall provided "pretty girls and lots of fun." Shortly after opening, it was renamed the Figaro, with an entrance on D Street. The function of Piper's investment is clear; the Figaro (née Alhambra) offered an enticement for lonely men with female companionship as entertainment—a place of assignation.

German immigrant Dick Bermann had been a bartender at Piper's corner saloon and the Opera House, and the *Gold Hill News* believed he knew how to "run such a saloon properly," implying the dancing led to paid sexual encounters between the dance hall girls and the men who visited the hall. Apparently, he knew something of the power of the press also, as he presented one reporter of the *Enterprise* with a huge keg of lager after four days in his new job.

Even with supportive reviews from the local papers, the Figaro business was short-lived, as arsonist activity resulted in the loss of the building in a fire by early 1871. Presumably John Piper had created local enemies with his takeover of the competition. Edmund Leathes, a supporting actor, estimated that seven different arson attempts on Piper's Opera House occurred during 1870 and 1871. Piper countered the arsonists by assuming chairmanship of the local vigilante committee.

Conflicts between arsonists and vigilante forces composed of local businessmen with much at stake continued throughout 1871, which saw numerous fires and a fluid cast of characters as antagonists. In later years, actor McKee Rankin stated that he had witnessed the murder of William Smith by Arthur Perkins at the International Hotel on March 5, 1871, which ultimately led to the murder of Perkins by the "601" vigilantes of Virginia City. Rankin believed he had witnessed Perkins being strung up in the basement of the Opera House and then shot. Alf Doten's journal clarifies that twenty-four-year-old Perkins, a piano player at Scott's dance saloon, cruised town as a "sport" and a participant in a lot of "rows." The contemporary reports

The Frederick Hotel (*right*) was built on the location of the old Alhambra. Notice how the hotel runs from C Street to D Street along the significant slope. *Fourth Ward School Museum Archives, McGinty Collection, Virginia City, NV.*

assert the vigilantes took Perkins directly to the Ophir Mine. In 1898, Doten explained Perkins's death in detail: Perkins was marched to the old Ophir works above A Street, "to the trestle of a mining car track, stood…up on a short piece of plank placed across the track, his arms and legs tied, and a stout rope leading from his neck to a beam overhead. Then they kindly advised him to give a good jump straight up, when they would remove or turn away the plank, thus allowing him a clear, effective drop down through the rails. He approved the grim utility of the idea, and the last words of Arthur Perkins, as he gave a vigorous, resolute spring upward, were: 'Turn her loose, boys!'" On his back, a placard appeared to credit the "601" with the deed, the first time this designation was used by the vigilantes.

Not all of the drama appeared onstage at Piper's Opera House, as William Willis "sparred" his way into the theater on March 11, 1871, only to be summarily ordered out by John Piper. Piper and others heard Willis threaten to "get even" with him, according to newspaper reports. Years later, Willis recalled being "jerked" on the shoulder by Piper and forcibly told to get out. Willis said he went upstairs and purchased a ticket, which he handed to Piper, who was then standing at the bar. Willis recalled: "I said, 'Here is your ticket; I don't want to see your show, either.'" The next night, Willis snuck into the theater through an open window and spread coal oil over the "wood and rubbish there and touched it off with a match," as the local papers reported. With coal oil on his hands and the sleeves of his coat, Willis was arrested. Unsatisfied with traditional justice, the vigilante committee,

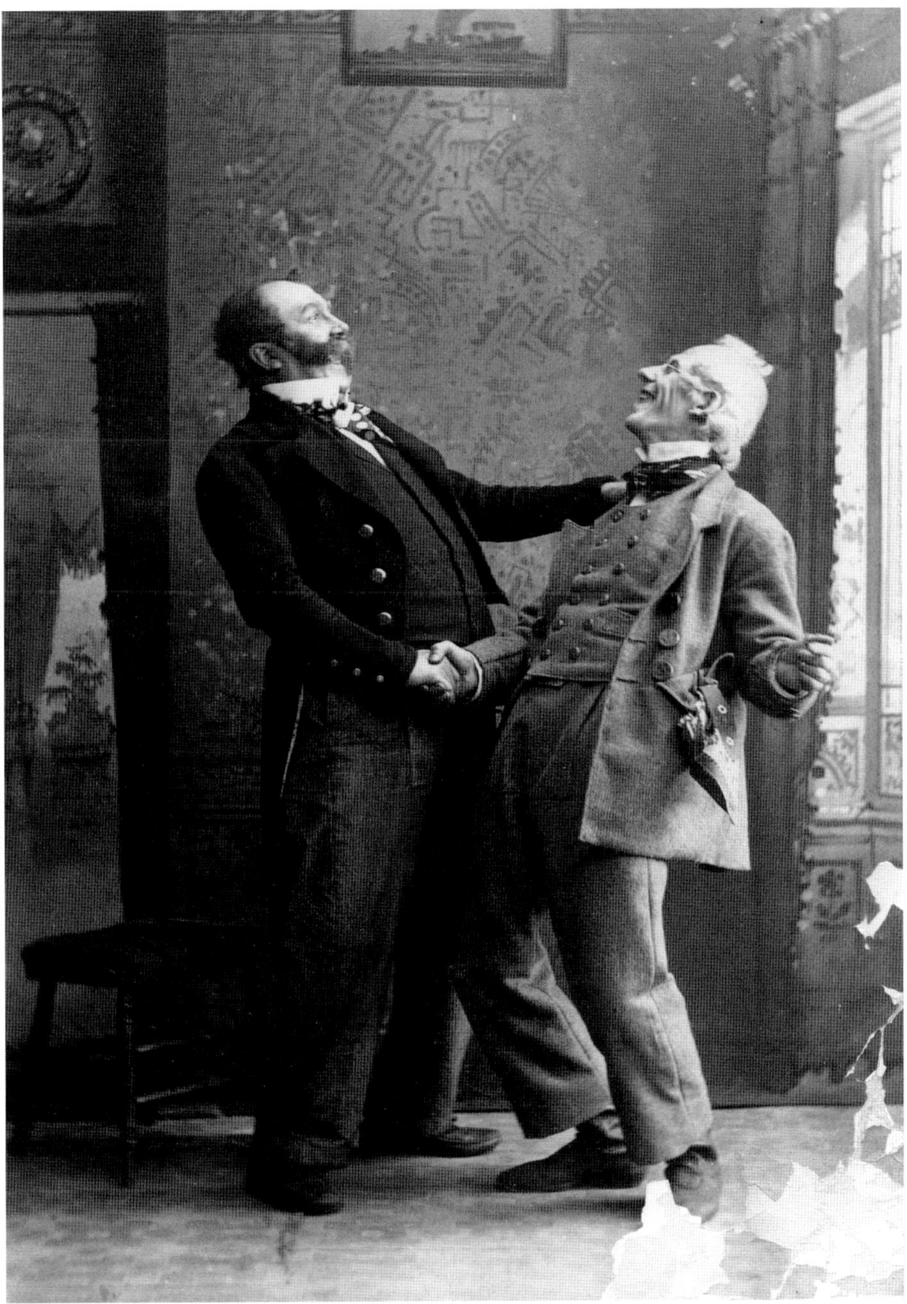

McKee Rankin (*left*) with an unidentified actor. He confused the details of the arsonist activities when relating his memories as an older man. He had a successful career on the stage and in theater management. *Author's collection.*

in their first act outside the law, took William Willis from his jail cell to the basement of the Opera House and put a rope around his neck. Then they put the rope over a beam, which was in full view of the embers of his incendiary attempt the night before. With the rope around his neck, Willis confessed to the arson and reported that the murderer Arthur Perkins was the arsonist responsible for the recent Athletic Hall fire, as well as other fires and attempts that had occurred earlier in the year. Then he also named two other accomplices who had accompanied them on a drunken incendiary rampage. Willis was later sentenced to twenty-one years in prison by the district court, after having pleaded guilty to arson in the first degree. When Willis came up for parole in 1876, the *Enterprise* argued against his claim that he had been forced into this confession, noting he did not deny the veracity of the events. Both Perkins and Willis were members of the same volunteer fire department and apparently co-conspirators in the rash of arsons that plagued the city. Virginia City's first "great fire," in late 1871 threatened the Opera House and consumed about one-third of the southern part of the city. Another arsonist, George Kirk, was treated to a neck-tie sociable, as the *Gold Hill News* termed it, which presumably ended the arsonist activity. Few arsonist attacks were reported after 1872.

8

THE DEPRESSION YEARS CONTINUE

BULLS, BEARS, WILDCATS, PIT BULLS, FEMALE MINSTRELS—ALL THAT GLITTERS IS NOT GOLD

Worst fraud I ever saw at that theater.
—complained Alf Doten in his journal after witnessing misidentified pictures of the Franco-Prussian War fail miserably from technical problems with the "powerful magnesium light"

The year 1871 was another borrasca year for the Opera House, as it hit a new low in programming with animal matches, including a bull and bear fight and wild cats fighting pit bulls. The Opera House reduced its theatrical offerings from June to November, suffering for six months without legitimate dramatic plays. When legitimate theater did occur, the offerings reflected programming agreements between John McCullough, who then managed San Francisco's California Theater, and John Piper. The East Coast actors McCullough drew to San Francisco made stops in Sacramento and Virginia City, creating a regional circuit for those traveling stars. During the depressed years, mid-1869 to early 1874, many different traveling performers stopped at Piper's, usually for short engagements. Supporting actors from San Francisco's California Theater presented starring roles in Virginia City as a way to practice their craft. By 1871, San Francisco's *Figaro* newspaper had observed that John Piper had "got" Virginia City, meaning his strategies—including buying the competition—secured the prominence of his Opera House in the town's theatrical world.

Opera was considered very high-class and respectable. Attendance at operatic music events reflected positively on audience members. Occasionally,

Adelaide Phillips, one of the few contraltos to attain national recognition during this time. *Author's collection.*

operatic singers performed in concert or presented portions of operas to the more elevated patrons. Adelaide Phillips first toured the Far West in 1865, while employed as part of an operatic company by Tom Maguire for his Academy of Music theater. Her 1870 tour found an expansion into small towns, including Virginia City, where Phillips drew elite audiences. Moderate success with the first two Virginia City shows compelled Phillips to then offer a concert of sacred music, which prompted the *Gold Hill News* to comment, "We don't believe the greatest female singer mentioned in sacred history, backed up by Beethoven and old Dr. Watts, could draw anything more than a corporal's guard in the way of an audience at a sacred concert in Virginia City." Phillips returned to Maguire's San Francisco Opera House, never again to return to the mining town.

Supporting players from San Francisco became stars on Piper's stage. Born into a theatrical family, Emilie Melville began her career as a five-year-old playing the Duke of York to Edwin Forrest's Richard III. She moved to San Francisco in 1868, joining the California Theater company as an ingénue when the theater opened the following year, eventually

Left: California Theater supporting actress Emilie Melville became a leading lady on the Comstock. *Author's collection.*

Right: Actor Edwin Adams. *Author's collection.*

displacing Annette Ince as the leading lady. She remained a popular actress there for a few years and frequently toured to Virginia City, where she could take leading roles that were above her status in California. While at the California Theater, Melville studied fine opera, allowing her debut as an operatic star. She then perfected the craft on a tour to Australia, eventually establishing her own opéra bouffe company that operated from 1881 to 1883.

John McCullough frequently stopped in Virginia City when traveling east, even if he didn't have a scheduled engagement at the theater. In February 1871, actor John T. Raymond, the low comedian of the California Theater under McCullough, performed in Virginia City in starring roles, as had Emilie Melville. McCullough proceeded to the footlights to recite at Raymond's benefit show. Densely packed audiences found fellow actor Edwin Adams as a member. Seated in a front box, Adams joked at McCullough's expense. With the loud applause dying down, Adams reached way over the box's edge and started another round of applause for McCullough. McCullough began reciting a poem written by Bret Harte, "In the Tunnel," which starts with

Character actor and quick-change artist William Horace Lingard costumed as a woman. *Author's collection.*

"Didn't know Flynn—Flynn of Virginia." Adams stood up, pantomimed and raised his hand as if to ask a question; then he shook his head. "He was sorry, perhaps it was all his fault, but he did not know Flynn of Virginia," he mouthed in pantomime. McCullough started again, and Adams again stood and shook his head. The audience roared. McCullough waited for the audience to calm down and started again. Adams again pantomimed his denial, making it funnier each time. "McCullough, at a complete loss, turned his back on his audience, got control of his face, then turned around and said: 'And that's all I know of Flynn of Virginia,'" and then walked off the stage, according to the memories of fellow actor William Crane. The somber poem about a miner named Tom Flynn saving the life of another miner in a mine accident, was assumed to have been set in Virginia City. Unfortunately, the brilliant comic actor Edwin Adams became sick while on tour and passed away six years later.

The small, nervous and temperamental actor William Horace Lingard carried a two-night run in 1871 in comedic impersonations of women and famous people, including President Grant and Brigham Young. London-born Lingard came to New York in 1868, bringing his native music hall comedy and music to American audiences. He focused on quick costume changes and farces, and his comedy song with nonsensical lyrics "Captain Jinx of the Horse Marines" was interspersed with comedy patter and became a mainstay of his act. While he traveled with his wife, Alice Dunning, and only two other supporting cast members, his impersonations were interspersed with light comedy skits by the other members of the troupe. He returned in 1875 and 1881. In 1875, Alice was reminded by the *Enterprise* that she could receive her accolades from either the parquette or the dress circle. She had performed some bit of theatrical business that appeared undignified and unwomanly, apparently rewarded by only the cheering parquette—the seating area for rowdy young men—in a comment which demonstrates that class divisions in performance as well as seating were important.

Sue Robinson, considered the best comedic actress in the West, was taken by death in 1871 at the age of twenty-six, despite having performed only weeks prior at Piper's Opera House. She had spent more than twenty years in show business in the West, taking perhaps three hundred different roles in her lifetime. She came to California as a child "fairy star" performing with her family for Gold Rush miners, and then she settled in Virginia City with her husband and two sons to become the leading lady at Piper's Opera House. At the height of her career, she created her own

Alice Dunning, Lingard's wife, enjoyed her own notoriety and successes in the theater in legitimate plays. *Author's collection.*

Actress Sue Robinson, costumed for a play. This photograph was taken in Carson City only weeks before her death. *History Room, California State Library, Sacramento, CA.*

touring company and was planning to get a job in one of Chicago's best theaters when she died unexpectedly. Her last role was in a play called *Ambition*, a title that illuminates the emotion that drove most actresses' lives. Buried in Sacramento's New Helvetica Cemetery, Sue Robinson's tombstone read, "A fallen rose, the fairest, sweetest but most transient of all the lovely sisterhood," giving a sense of the fleeting nature of the acting profession and the ephemeral status of the characters created by the stage. But celebrity status created pitfalls. In the late 1880s, a disillusioned fan who could not believe that Sue had died attempted to disinter Sue's body, prompting the family to relocate her grave.

Sue Robinson's popularity emanated from her status as a local favorite, but several important national stars also appeared at the Opera House during the depression years. Early in 1871, character actor Joseph K. Emmet played Piper's for four nights. Arriving in San Francisco under an engagement with the California Theater, Emmett's vehicle, *Fritz, Our Cousin*

Joseph K. Emmet tobacco card. *Author's collection.*

German, a four-act play, was first produced in New York in 1870 for a grand sixty-three performances. Emmett was considered the creator of the genre of the German dialect role. It became Emmett's lifelong signature characterization, and by 1871, it had earned him the title "most successful star in the country" from the *Enterprise*. The story of German immigrant Fritz, who faced adversity in America, exemplified his ability to still hold true to traditional family values. The play combined elements of vaudeville with melodrama and underscored Yankee ingenuity. Emmett's talent lay in his good eye for character, a wealth of broad humor and vocal flexibility. Emmett became rich and famous from the role that showed America could both profit from and improve upon the lives of immigrants.

Emmett played to good audiences with attendance from ladies in near record-setting numbers. On his last night in Virginia City, Joseph Emmet made a speech to the audience at the end of the last curtain call. He had been advised not to come to Virginia City, as he would not be appreciated. He did not believe the admonishment and came anyway. He felt rewarded for his presentations and would "always think most kindly of the friendly people he had met here." The fact that the theatrical fraternity had advised him against Piper's Opera House provides insight into contemporary stories of the difficult reception some players received. The town had developed some notoriety among performers for having problematic audiences, and many actors apparently shunned the mining town. A few weeks before Emmett's run, actor Daniel Bandmann's play had been stopped by the young men in the parquette playing cowbells, tin horns and trumpets. By 1873, J.K. Emmett had received 70 percent of the gross receipts in Augustin Daly's New York theater, an unheard-of amount, based in part on this successful Western tour. He then performed the role of Fritz more than two thousand times for American audiences.

Another high point of 1871 occurred with the appearance of the Hyers sisters from Sacramento. Only teenagers, Anna Madah and Emma Louise had opened in their hometown of Sacramento in 1867 as child prodigies. By 1876, the Hyers Sisters Combination constituted one of the earliest professional Black theater companies in America, producing musical comedies that demonstrated Black Americans could equal white Americans in any undertaking. Expanding their musical repertoire to include spirituals, camp songs and sentimental ballads, the Hyers sisters' show became a national institution for almost three decades as it established the groundwork for American Black musical theater. The ladies' 1876 production of *Out of Bondage* allowed gifted artists to perform in vehicles that affirmed human dignity and professional training. They returned to Nevada in 1879 in *Out of Bondage*, and in 1888, when Emma performed in *Uncle Tom's Cabin.*

The Hyers sisters. *Billy Rose Theatre Collection, New York Public Library.*

After November 1871, shows from San Francisco came to Nevada for one-week engagements during a short closure at the California Theater. These short runs included John McCullough and Frank Chanfrau. The handsome Chanfrau was toward the end of a long career when he performed on the Comstock. He had come to California in 1851, bringing an innovative character based on a New York bowery boy, Mose. Later, he distinguished himself in Eastern and Midwestern theaters, being exceptionally popular at McVicker's in Chicago, where he appeared ten times from 1857 to 1871. Known for his dark eyes and dark curly hair, he impersonated Mose and, later, Sam in plays by the same names for nearly twenty years, and he became famous for developing the tough city kid personality.

In Virginia City, *Sam* played for two nights, and then Chanfrau switched to *Kit, the Arkansas Traveler*. The actor had added *Kit* to his repertoire in 1870, and it served him well for twelve consecutive seasons. Kit Redding, as Chanfrau's creation, became the everyman pioneer. With many plot twists

Frank Chanfrau, costumed as Sam for the play of the same name. *Author's collection.*

and a spectacular Mississippi River steamboat shipwreck on a small island, the play was well received by audiences who had missed that type of spectacle drama for the past six months, with the well-rehearsed supporting company finally up to the task. The new scenic designer worked for two weeks on the scenic effects. May Howard, the new leading lady of the California Theater supported Chanfrau's tour.

It was a lackluster year in programming, with San Francisco stars highlighting the dependency that Piper's had on the theaters there. From opera singers to pugilistic grizzly bears, the theater attempted to be all things to all people, but little artistic direction can be attributed to John Piper, as he leased the theater to others, and their entertainment penchants held

Brunette May Howard served as a leading lady at the California Theater from August 1870 to May 1872 and also intermittently performed at Piper's Opera House. *Author's collection.*

forth. Piper drew acts from Tom Maguire's theaters and John McCullough's California Theater, which supplied the most lucrative shows.

The first legitimate drama of 1872 did not occur until May, under the management of John McCullough and John Piper as joint proprietors. In the face of economic recession, Piper had created a removable dance floor to allow for roller-skating, local club dances and get-togethers, as there were long breaks between professional artists. The opening months of the year welcomed minstrel shows and visiting lecturers. Then in March, the longest Opera House engagement lasted for eight weeks, brought by possibly the least respectable troupe of performers, the Amelia Dean Female Minstrels. Amelia Dean's assemblage opened with thirty male and female performers

Pauline Cushman served as a Northern spy during the Civil War and traveled as a lecturer after the war. *Special Collections Photograph, UNRS-P0209-4.tif collection_6555; Special Collections and University Archive Collections, University of Nevada, Reno.*

in flimsy costumes performing salacious skits and gymnastic routines. The "neat little bar in the green room" facilitated the ability of audience members to meet the "sociable young damsels connected with the troupe," opined the *Gold Hill News*. At least two of the young women of the troupe ended their lives a few months later, after experiencing employment in one of the local legal brothels on D Street. Charles Wheatleigh returned in June, and later in the year, John McCullough returned with his mistress, Helen Tracy, in the cast. Lawrence Barrett returned for only one week when his closing play *Divorce* brought large audiences of respectable women who were interested in the subject.

The years after the Civil War experienced a shift from public lectures for intellectual enlightenment to lectures as popular entertainment, and some notable women speakers, including Elizabeth Cady Stanton, Edith O'Gorman, Mrs. Joaquin Miller and Major Pauline Cushman, a Northern Civil War spy, spoke to the locals from the stage of Piper's Opera House. Women lecturers brought gender issues to Virginia City audiences, shaping popular opinion at theaters, the purview of entertainers, rather than libraries and fraternal societies. Newspaperman Alf Doten escorted Ms. Cushman around town for a few days before her lecture and met her in the theater green room before and after the lecture. He reported her speech a failure in his journal: "She is a poor speaker and she broke down at several times, lost her temper, etc.; Had evidently been taking whiskey, morphine, or something of the sort. In green room after lecture she cried bitterly." He escorted her back to her room at the International Hotel and continued, "I was in her room with her for an hour or so—didn't invite me to [erasure] and so I didn't—Left at 12." Alf Doten loaned Cushman money to pay her boarding bill and offered her sandwiches and a small bottle of cocktails on her departure from Nevada. Other speakers were more successful.

Blind Tom began performing as a child while still enslaved. He was the most frequently observed variety performer on American stages for much of the 1800s. *Billy Rose Theatre Collection, New York Public Library.*

Blind Tom, who was in his early twenties when he played Piper's in 1873, had a forty-year career on the stage that ended in the twentieth century in vaudeville shows. An autistic savant born into slavery in 1849, Tom was kept in a guardianship by his enslavers, and he and his biological family profited little from his talent. Blind Tom's schedule of up to thirty-five piano concerts a month for nine months of the year for most of his life made him one of the most well-known performers in America and one of the country's most important musical personalities of the late nineteenth century. At Piper's Opera House, he played "Fisher's Hornpipe" with one hand and "Yankee Doodle" with the other hand in another key, while concurrently singing "Tramp, Tramp, Tramp" in yet a different key. He could imitate sounds he heard and replay any music played for him by other musicians who attempted to challenge his ability to "play by ear." He also created and published his own compositions.

Precocious child star Fay Templeton delighted audiences in a long theatrical career.
Author's collection.

Panic on the Comstock over mining stock drops, mine companies leveling assessments on stockholders rather than paying dividends, and the general malaise from the national Panic of 1873 all put a damper on theatergoers' thoughts. Some entertainers were able to relieve the stress of audiences and help them forget their troubles for a few moments. Actor Sheil Barry, while on a rare Western tour, performed in comedy shows, including *Dust and Diamonds*, *His Last Legs*, *Rory O'More* and *The Happy Man*, billed as a "laughable comedy, a sensational drama and a roaring extravaganza" by the *Gold Hill News* in November 1873. In later years, Barry became known for taking sympathetic Irish roles in plays in England and Australia.

Monday, December 8, 1873, saw a "Grand Triple Alliance" of James A. Herne, returning to the Comstock for one week with eight-year-old Fay Templeton and her actress mother, Alice Vane. Child star Fay Templeton was the hit of the show and remained an American institution for a grand sixty-four-year career. Known for her exuberant clowning and throaty-voiced singing, Templeton played in vaudeville well into the twentieth century, becoming the principal soubrette of Weber and Fields's New York music hall as an adult. This stop in Virginia City was part of an American tour that brought Templeton national fame by the age of fifteen. In her early twenties, she fought censorship of her daring costumes.

Before the discovery of the Big Bonanza in late 1873, Virginia City floundered in depressed straights financially, and the theater programming reflected lesser-known artists. A heavy dependence on Irish performers, as well as Irish material throughout 1873, may reflect a desire to appeal to the substantial Irish population. More than six performances of *The New Magdalen*, or parts of the play, along with three presentations of *Camille* by different leading actresses, may also argue for the importance of the demimonde to the financial success of the theater.

The Panic of 1873 in the East drove performers west. The big bonanza ore chamber strike late in 1873 brought relatively good times to the West, and as long as that ore held out, the West did not feel the Panic. Also in 1873, the federal government issued a policy that was to become known as the "Crime of '73." That policy demonetized silver, and the government stopped buying all produced silver—purchasing only small amounts—which eventually led to the end of the dominance the silver mining concerns had enjoyed. For theater, 1874 became a banner year.

9

BONANZA YEARS PRODUCE STARS, STARS, STARS

There is scarcely a page in the history of Virginia City before the fire [1875] *that would not make lurid melodrama too strong for the palate of the Theatre-goer of today.*
—said David Belasco, My Life's Story, *1914*

The Big Bonanza ore chamber strike in the Consolidated Virginia Mine in 1873 brought prosperity—but not until late in the year. Its effect was primarily realized in 1874. After the Big Bonanza discovery, Piper's attained its greatest devotion to legitimate theater with a large, talented stock company of international players. With this new ore discovery, the Comstock boomed back into good times, and programming for the new year reflected the change, allowing Piper's Opera House to draw on the multitude of talents at John McCullough's California Theater. Appearing in both venues were Agnes Perry Booth and her husband, Junius Brutus Booth Jr.; Lotta Crabtree; John T. Raymond; Katherine Rogers; Frank Mayo; Dion Boucicault; Kate Denin; Mrs. Henrietta Chanfrau; Amy Stone and William Florence. Most of these stars enjoyed a month's run in California, compared to a week at Piper's, but every major star this year had come from or was going to the California Theater in San Francisco. John Piper's goal, to equal San Francisco's entertainment, came closest to achievement in 1874 and 1875. Virginia City earned its theatrical ranking as second only to San Francisco on the West Coast.

The bonanza found in the Consolidated Virginia Mine spread underground to other mines on the Comstock Lode, increasing not only total mining output but also stock speculation. Money was plentiful, as one mine's payroll for a week totaled $80,000. The bonanza times were characterized by national talents and by more continuous programming without significant breaks in engagements between players. Less time was spent using the Opera House for community events and lectures, but the lecturers reflected a higher level of notoriety than previously witnessed. Two prominent speakers, Victoria Woodhull and Adolph Sutro, who lectured twice this year, attracted large audiences. As theatrical tastes changed, the last true minstrel show at Piper's appeared in 1874.

Virginia City became more sedate, ascribing to more staid Victorian standards. The town fathers, concerned about the evils of the red-light district, considered a ban on the sex trade within the city limits. The paper noted the loss of brothel property by the expansion of the Virginia & Truckee Railroad depot and that, in grading the ground for its warehouses, sidings and depot, the railroad had done more for the eradication of the profession than the aldermen did through legislation.

The great Dublin-born dramatist Dion Boucicault opened a four-night run in his own *Kerry* with a fat leading role. Immense audiences attended despite February's cold winter weather. After ending a month in San Francisco and a four-night Sacramento run, Boucicault appeared at California's capital city under Piper's management, where prices for reserved seating were increased, a testament to Boucicault's star power. The second night of his engagement brought John McCullough for one last performance in Virginia City, perhaps to ensure his success and his place in the hearts of the mining town population. Dion Boucicault offered his own creations, *Colleen Bawn* and *Arrah-Na-Pogue*, and then *Daddy O'Dowd*, another Irish-themed play, for the last night. The heartbreaking story of the Irish farmer who must sell his farm to save his American child brought tears to almost the entire audience. The works of Boucicault had broad-based appeal to immigrants and nativists alike due to the emotion of the plays rather than the intellectual arguments.

The violent storm on February 13 did not deter attendance to see Kate Denin in *East Lynne*. *The Child Stealer* and *Sea of Ice* were followed by *Under the Gaslight* as the main vehicle for Kate Denin's benefit show. The *Geneva Cross*, which enjoyed a long run in New York, rounded out the bill for the actress who had performed on stage since childhood. Newspaperman Alf Doten and his new wife witnessed *Under the Gaslight*, starring Denin, whom

Left: Dublin-born Dion Bouccicault, costumed for a role in one of his own plays. *Author's collection.*

Right: Actress Kate Denin. *Author's collection.*

he didn't like. "Too big and coarse," he criticized her to his journal, but his newspaper's reviews placed Kate Denin on the short list of best living actresses. Kate Denin would stay on at Piper's in support of Katherine Rogers's roles as leading lady, giving credibility to the theater's claim of having an outstanding supporting company.

Katherine Rogers, from the Drury Lane Theater in London and formerly a leading lady with Wallack's in New York, opened Piper's as "one of the best [actresses] ever here," according to Alf Doten's journal. With a theater crowded to its utmost capacity, with all aisles full, the talented lady received a brick of pure silver bullion engraved with a stage, lyre, volume of Shakespeare, footlights and this blessing: "Presented to Miss Katherine Rogers by her friends, Virginia City, Nevada March 2, 1874." The front of the brick had an engraved couplet from *Romeo and Juliet*: "Her beauty hangs upon the cheek of night / Like a rich jewel in Ethiop's ear," reported the *Gold Hill News*.

Led Astray, written by Dion Boucicault for Katherine Rogers, his mistress, depicted a story of romantic affairs by spouses caught in a passionless

Left: Actress Katherine Rogers. *Author's collection.*

Right: Victoria Woodhull, the first woman to run for president, drew large crowds for her lectures. *Billy Rose Theatre Collection, New York Public Library.*

marriage. It became the most famous drama of its decade in America and completed almost five hundred performances in London, helping usher in more realistic theater. Rogers returned to Piper's in 1875, when she took leading roles in *The Hunchback*; *Leah, the Forsaken* and *Romeo and Juliet*.

Attracting upper-class Comstock women, Victoria Woodhull, one of the most powerful speakers of the era, lectured on May 18 to a crowded house. Victoria Woodhull was the first woman to run for president, doing so in 1872. Acting out the most extreme positions on a public stage, she demanded female equality, including advocacy for mechanical birth control. A remarkable character who manipulated the press to keep her ideas before the public, she contributed to change in the Victorian era by challenging notions of gender and class. Her national lecture tours drew an estimated half a million people during the mid-1870s. In Virginia City, Woodhull's criticism of the White House brought a "dress circle Republican" filled with "Democratic whisky" to attempt an interruption, deftly squelched by Woodhull, who drew on spirituality and prescience in delivering her polemic on societal changes. She did not "discourse in disguised metaphor or obscure

Left: Actress Henrietta Chanfrau, wife of Frank Chanfrau, excelled in a national theatrical career. *Library of Congress.*

Opposite: Actress Agnes Booth rose from melodeon dancer to become a celebrated actress. *Author's collection.*

language," and although many may not have agreed with her message, no one was "injured" by listening to the lecture. "Sensible people can always listen to square talk and honest argument with more or less profit," opined the *Gold Hill News*.

With bonanza times on the Comstock, the number of attractions increased; dances, lectures and fraternal organization events were potentially able to take a toll on the attendance at the Opera House. Only a remarkable, stellar performer could hope to attract densely packed houses for a performance. One actress able to do that was Henrietta Chanfrau. She opened on October 5, 1874, in *Was She Right?—A Question for Women*, which explores the perils of motherhood. The womanly roles of Mrs. Chanfrau dominated the Opera House for a one-week run, recognizing changing audience priorities and the importance of women as audience members. She presented *Jealousy*, a tear-jerker, and *The Wife's Stratagem* to densely seated audiences. Contemporary newspapers do not mention her performing in any theaters other than the California and

Left: Junius Brutus Booth Jr. *Library of Congress.*

Opposite: William Florence, a celebrated Irish American character actor, was one of the most successful comedians of his time. Pictured in *No Thoroughfare. Victoria and Albert Museum Archive.*

Piper's on this Pacific coast tour. As the wife of actor Frank S. Chanfrau, she had a noteworthy career of her own, which brought her acclaim as one of the most refined and intelligent actresses on the stage and saw her manage a New Orleans theater for one season. Mrs. Chanfrau toured the Consolidated Virginia Mine before embarking on her next engagement in St. Louis. It was a common practice to host visiting celebrities on mining tours. John Piper often personally provided tours for his stars.

Agnes Booth, the wife of Junius Brutus Booth Jr., brought her best roles to Piper's in 1874, although her San Francisco tour had lasted only twelve days to a mixed audience response. Australian-born Agnes Booth appeared with Maguire's San Francisco Opera House stock company as early as 1858, completing a difficult Virginia City engagement, which included her fancy dance routine at Topliffe's melodeon. Her six-year apprenticeship with Tom Maguire allowed Mrs. Booth to develop a multitude of talents, support Adah Isaacs Menken's tour and help open the original Maguire's Virginia City Opera House as a supporting player in 1863. In 1874, Agnes was praised for bringing back Shakespeare when she added *Romeo and Juliet* and *Much Ado About Nothing* to her play list. Her other leading roles in *Lady of Lyons*, *The Hunchback* and *Elene* saw new scenery built especially for her shows. "June" Booth Jr. died in 1883, and Agnes went on to greater fame

and recognition, far surpassing her husband in her histrionic abilities in the minds of national critics.

Junius "June" Brutus Booth Jr. was the oldest son in a notorious acting family, fathered by the famous antebellum actor Junius Booth. He received lesser notoriety than both Edwin and John Wilkes Booth, his famous brothers. June performed at the opening of Maguire's Opera House in 1863, after serving in theater management in San Francisco during the 1850s. In 1874, Booth offered two performances of *King John*, often considered his best role, for Virginia City's audiences. Australian-born stage manager Willie Gill presented two of his own compositions before another nationally known thespian, W.J. Florence, appeared.

The end of the California Theater's season on December 12 allowed William "W.J." Florence to open two days later in Virginia City with *Dombey and Son*, based on Charles Dickens's work, for a six-night run. He appeared with support from Piper's stock company, which local newspapers considered the best in memory. W.J. Florence, toward the middle of his career, when he trod the boards at Piper's, first appeared professionally in New York in 1850. Florence had been performing in *Ticket-of-Leave Man* since 1863, when he opened in New York in the titular role, later presenting it for thousands of nights throughout the country. With gritty scenes of vice and coarseness, the protagonist, a trusting prison parolee, is made a fall guy for a group of counterfeiters. Florence, whose career began as a teenager supporting a fatherless family, spoofed Washington corruption in his caricature of a vulgar Yankee politician in *The Mighty Dollar*. W.J. Florence and his wife brought his signature creation in *The Mighty Dollar* to Piper's second opera house in March 1879 for four nights with one matinee engagement, during which he repeated *Ticket-of-Leave Man* and added *No Thoroughfare*.

Boredom with variety shows crept into the newspaper reviews. The people wanted stars, and variety shows suffered. First-class actors have always drawn large audiences in this community, posited the *Gold Hill News*, as the policy of drawing on California for players continued in 1875. Many stars from the California Theater again graced the stage at Piper's. Katherine Rogers; Lawrence Barrett; Mrs. D.P. Bowers; James O'Neill; William Mestayer; Dominick Murray; Little Nell, The California Diamond, a local who became famous internationally; and Bella Pateman, the California Theater's leading lady, all took their turn at the footlights. Two- and three-week engagements demonstrate the attraction of legitimate dramas for Virginia City audiences, as both Little Nell and Katherine Rogers achieved wide acclaim. Two-week engagements for Lawrence

Barrett and Mrs. D.P. Bowers also demonstrate a change in the population with the improved economy. Audiences with more disposable income, a greater desire to attend the theater and a generalized move toward elevated programming for respectable women took precedent in 1875. Similarly, the local Paiutes experienced such a high level of acculturation that they not only appreciated the theater as playgoers, but they also participated as performers, a phenomenon noted for the first time in 1874. They supported Cuban-born Marie Zoe in *Wept of the Wish-ton-Wish.*

Excited audiences welcomed the return of a local favorite, Little Nell, who was born in San Francisco but raised in Gold Hill. She was nationally known as The California Diamond. Born Nellie Gibson, Nell appeared at age five under Tom Maguire's management, becoming a melodeon performer at the Gold Hill Theater. In 1865, she appeared at Maguire's Opera House in Virginia City with Matilda Heron. She returned in 1867 at eight years old. On the short list of nationally recognized "dramatic prodigies," Little Nell became a talent who mimicked Lotta Crabtree. In January 1875, a select audience filled seats, steps and aisles of the dress circle for *No Name*, a play written especially for the star. Many were turned away, as even the space for "standing room" was filled. Little Nell was on her way to San Francisco's California Theater, where she would be supported by William Mestayer, who received the California newspaper's praise. Audiences there would be attending for Mestayer. Nell's popularity in Virginia City, originating from her previous local residence, was not maintained in the Bay City. Nell's blackface impressions, sung in a deep voice in "Who's Dat a-Knocking?" show a level of provincialism that may not have been appreciated in the more sophisticated San Francisco, which, by this time, found interest in minstrelsy waning. As Helen Dauvray, Little Nell became characterized in the 1880s as "a really finished…actress of high comedy," to quote Odell's *Annuals of the New York Stage.*

The leading lady of the California Theater, Bella Pateman, possessed a "youthful figure" and "great beauty of face," with the force and intensity to match the artistry of John McCullough in San Francisco's *Macbeth*, according to the *Daily Alta California*. But only thirty ladies attended Bella Pateman's opening night at Piper's in *The New Magdalen*. Perhaps the subject matter of the play—compassion and redemption for fallen women—created "a natural prejudice against the class suggested by the title of the play" and influenced people against attending, believed the *Gold Hill News*. After repeating *Magdalen*, the star brought out *Article 47*, which challenged Pateman's range of emotion with an electrifying mad scene in which the

Left: British-born Bella Pateman, a leading lady at the California Theater in early 1875, became a starring actress when in Nevada. *Victoria and Albert Museum Archive.*

Right: London-born Sydney Cowell and her husband, George Giddens, were part of the supporting company at Piper's from January through May 1875 after experiencing successes in San Francisco. *Author's collection.*

Creole beauty Cora's predicaments end in raving madness. *Article 47* was offered for two nights. Pateman continued with plays that appealed to respectable women.

John Piper cast his supporting players, including Sydney Cowell and her husband, adrift in May and brought in three touring companies with complete casts and sets. It foretold the wave of the future. Cowell eventually became an actress with Daly's New York theater, where she performed for the rest of her life. But first, a winsome Alice Oates, in a spicy opéra bouffe with a cast of twenty-eight, thrilled audiences. Opéra bouffe had replaced legitimate opera in many American theaters by the mid-1870s, and the Oates group was only one of many proponents of this trend, finding their greatest success from 1876 to 1883.

Three noteworthy complete touring companies entertained this year, as the trend toward national touring "combination companies" began in

Starring winsome Alice Oates, her opéra bouffe troupe appeared with a full orchestra. They were held over for additional shows. *Society of California Pioneers.*

James O'Neill came to Virginia City with the Hooley Company from Chicago. He's pictured here as the Count of Monte Cristo. *Library of Congress.*

earnest. Besides Oates's opéra bouffe were Hooley's from Chicago and Augustin Daly's Fifth Avenue troupe from New York City. These complete touring theatricals are an example of what would have continued—the age of complete traveling combination productions—for the Opera House, had it survived the Great Fire of 1875.

The Hooley Comedy Company, including James O'Neill, followed the Oates group. James fathered Eugene O'Neill, the first American playwright to win a Nobel Prize in Literature. James, born in Ireland, made his stage debut in America in 1868, after struggling against poverty. Known to one critic as an "exceptionally capable actor," O'Neill made his New York debut in 1876 and then returned to San Francisco as the Savior in *The Passion Play*, as well as other shows. O'Neill was arrested in 1879 for this portrayal of Christ in one of the fiercest controversies in San Francisco's theatrical history. Eugene O'Neill immortalized his father in his award-winning *Long Day's Journey into Night*, with a searing account of the pain-racked family. James's fear of poverty drove him to specialize in one role, Dantès in the *Count of Monte Cristo*, from 1883 onward. It imprisoned James's talent but provided pecuniary reward.

Nationally known talent Fanny Davenport appeared in an all-star cast with Augustin Daly's Fifth Avenue Theatre Company, which offered a short four-show engagement. John Drew starred with supporting players, including Maurice Barrymore, Mary Jeffries Lewis, James Lewis and Mrs. G.H. Gilbert. Able to showcase her abilities in high comedy, fine ladies' roles and coquettes, Davenport received rave reviews. Born into a theatrical family, Fanny began her career at the age of twelve. The star's brilliance in *Charity*, which she first undertook in 1874, earned an appreciation for her talent that would carry her throughout the century. Her success with Daly led her to leave his employ to establish her own touring company. In 1877, she starred under her own management, amassing huge financial success and popularity; her talent equaled her business acumen. In the 1880s and 1890s, Davenport acquired the American rights to four European plays famously performed there by Sarah Bernhardt. These tragedies,

Left: William Crane appeared with Hooley's Comedy Company early in his fifty-three-year career, that found him as half of a comedy duo with Stuart Robson. *Author's collection.*

Right: Fanny Davenport, one of the most beautiful actresses of the era, attained national fame and a lucrative career that placed her among the richest actresses of her time. *Author's collection.*

with lavish sets and costumes, secured her substantial wealth. She was one of the most famous and most successful actresses of the period to appear at Piper's.

Many of the supporting players deserve recognition for their exemplary careers. Mrs. Judah, née Marietta Starfield Torrence, specialized in character roles in an incredible career on the West Coast. As a character actress, Mrs. Judah was known for her professional, consistent work. Born in 1812 in New York, she died in 1883 after a more than thirty-year career on Western stages, working within a few months of her death. She arrived in San Francisco in 1852 with a tragic story of surviving a shipwreck that killed her husband and two children. Mrs. Judah floated on a piece of wood for days before being rescued. Suffering tragedy in her personal life, she excelled at comedy onstage. In her signature role as the Nurse in *Romeo*

Above: John Drew from Daly's New York City touring company is pictured here as Petruchio in Shakespeare's *The Taming of the Shrew*. *Author's collection*.

Opposite: Consummate supporting actors of the Daly theater were James Lewis and Mrs. G.H. Gilbert, who performed in 1875 in Virginia City. *Author's collection*.

and Juliet she personified adorable old age and overshadowed many Juliets, considered "the best old lady on the stage, personally or professionally," as the *San Jose Herald* claimed in 1878. She tantalized Romeo and displayed the perfect curiosity of an old woman of the lower class trying to determine his intentions toward her ward, Juliet. Her demeanor suggested her tragic life and the small, stocky, square-faced, stern-visaged actress became a fixture of the California Theater stock company from its inception in 1869 through 1878. Mrs. Judah married John Torrence, who had an extensive West Coast career backstage and in theater management. She spent a

Mrs. Judah (seated) as the nurse with Adelaide Neilson as Juliet in *Romeo and Juliet*. *Society of California Pioneers.*

lengthy career in San Francisco, supporting the major stars, and traveled to Virginia City with many, appearing there first in 1864. She supported John McCullough in his first Virginia City engagement in 1867, returning in 1870 in support of Lawrence Barrett and again in 1872 with the entire California Theater company.

10

THE "GREAT FIRE" NECESSITATES A NEW THEATER

John Piper of Virginia City, Nevada, a man then ignorant of theatrical matters, but with plenty of money, good-nature, and natural shrewdness. He played good people with fair success.
—Sacramento Daily Record-Union, *August 7, 1882*

Demonstrating extreme prescience, Virginia City's spiritualists predicted a huge fire almost a month before the actual event. Early in the morning of October 26, 1875, an unknown boarder at Crazy Kate Shay's on A Street accidentally knocked over an oil lamp, ending Virginia City as it was previously known. The arid tinderbox mining town on the side of Mount Davidson lost more than two-thirds of its wooden structures. The entire commercial district, including Piper's Opera House on D Street, Piper's Corner Saloon on B and Union Streets, both John and Henry Piper's personal homes, as well as the town's churches, stores, livery stables, mining headframes, brothels, saloons and residences were reduced to charcoal. Crazy Kate later denied any complicity with the event; Virginia City's Washoe Zephyr—the well-known, unpredictable high wind—was to blame.

Virginia City's Great Fire of 1875 ended the twelve-year-old theater on D Street. Even with huge water tanks posed on the Opera House roof and a fire hose within easy reach of the front door, firemen were at a loss when it came to saving the structure. "Piper's Opera House began to smoke and blaze.... Taking in the situation, Fire Chief White blew up the Opera House," rather than risk the spread to the railroad depot and mining structures, but to no avail, reported the *Sacramento Daily Union*. After the Opera House was dynamited, it "made a great and intensely hot fire," the *Enterprise* recalled. John Piper had left for San Francisco on October 21 under the rumor that he would need to replace A.D. Billings, one of the leading stock players, so he may have actually been absent from the town on the morning of the Great Fire. It is fitting that one of his last acts regarding the theater dealt with supporting player problems.

John Piper lost not only his Opera House and private home but also thirteen or fourteen other dwelling structures in Virginia City, totaling an estimated $65,000 to $75,000. What the *Enterprise* termed tenements, the *Gold Hill News* declared dwellings; presumably, the structures were brothels, as some lined D Street. The *Enterprise* believed most people depreciated their losses instead of inflating them. John Piper's losses ranked beneath those of the mines, mills, clothing stores with stock and the International Hotel, but at roughly $1.5 million in today's values, Piper's loss was one of the most extreme. He later built brothels on the site of the old Opera House on D Street, as the southern border of the legal red-light district moved south to Taylor Street.

By October 29, a contract had been let to enlarge the Carson City Theater, which Piper had been leasing since 1873, so Piper's large scenes and flats could fit into the structure. Piper lost no time making plans to continue in theatricals, as he had created a circuit of regional towns, including Carson City and Reno. Dressing rooms were added to the rear of the stage, and the newly remodeled Carson Theater would take over as "one of the best halls in the State," said the *Sacramento Daily Union*. John Piper lost his lease on the Metropolitan Theater in Sacramento due to the Great Fire, and by December, Piper's supporting company had disbanded, and it became impossible for him to put together another one, according to the Sacramento paper.

By the mid-1870s, times were changing. Respectability had won over the programming of the old Opera House. Respectable romantic love with virtue, self-control, sensibility and spirituality; wives performing their duties by caring for husbands and families; and principled behavior were much more common in the theatricalities presented on the stage. Increasingly, the behavior of drunkards, the demimonde and noisy audiences, as well as risqué spectacles gave way to finer drama in an atmosphere more like Victorian home parlors.

The new upwardly mobile business class dominated, with second-generation immigrants desperately striving to move into the middle class to gain respectability. These changes were reflected in the local newspapers, as the *Gold Hill News* published church service information, school events and strawberry socials, and lessened its coverage of the theater. Late in 1875, the reviews of the shows at Piper's decreased in column inch size in the *Gold Hill News*, while reviews of picnics, balls, the pioneer association, court proceedings and respectable happenings dominated. Innovations, such as the long run and darkened houselights during performances, helped turn playgoing into an aspect of consumerism. New elements included the private enjoyment of theatrical events rather than audience participation and public interaction with the stars. On the way out was the hooting, hollering and foot stomping of the earlier generations.

An interim time of almost three years ensued when Virginia City did not have a major theater, but performers still came to the mining town and performed in the miner's union hall, fraternal organization halls and other small venues. Virginia City was known as a good theater town, not only because it had become a significant industrialized city but also because of its demographics. John Piper could not give up on Virginia City, even as he must have witnessed numerous friends and neighbors leave the slopes of Mount Davidson.

Helena Modjeska became a respected nationally known actress. She played the mining town in 1877. *Author's collection.*

In 1877, William Cody, better known as Buffalo Bill, performed in Virginia City at the National Guard Hall in a play titled *The Scout of the Plains*, and then he continued at Carson City's theater. The real horses that were used onstage added to the thrill of the battle scenes. Cody returned to the new Piper's Opera House in 1879, appearing in *Knight of the Plains*, which earned a harsh comment from a local newspaper that labeled Cody a "bad actor." Buffalo Bill resigned from his lucrative ten-year career as an actor in legitimate theater to become the showman of Wild West shows, which held broad appeal to middle-class Americans.

Helena Modjeska also appeared at the National Guard Hall in 1877. One of Virginia City's most enduring stories concerns Modjeska, who toured underground in some of the leading mines. Upon her departure from one of the mines, she tipped her tour guide, a man dressed in rough shoes and muddy clothes, not realizing he was actually Nevada's Senator James Fair and the mine's owner. Modjeska first appeared in America in 1877, only one year after she left her native Poland. Mastering the English language to the point that she made stage appearances in Shakespearean plays demonstrates her intelligence, as well as energy and determination. By 1883, she was so well studied that she played Juliet to Edwin Booth's Romeo in his New York theater.

The new Piper's Opera House opened in January 1878, when it was rebuilt at the corner of B and Union Streets, incorporating the Piper's saloon and business block at that location, with John Piper as both its proprietor and manager. Exhibiting refined architecture, the new theater reflected the boom years of opulence and success, rather than the reduced state of affairs Virginia City would find itself in during the 1880s. John Piper filed for bankruptcy in mid-1878, which was complicated by a homestead on the property. After the resolution of the bankruptcy, John was listed as manager of the Opera House, although at various times, other theater managers were shown in advertisements for productions from their theaters. This theater lasted for five years and continued to host primarily touring companies.

The newly built Piper's Opera House opened with Ellie Wilton and Henry Edwards in *Shadows*, soon followed by *Camille* and *School for Scandal*. Both Wilton and Edwards, with some of the other supporting actors from the lost D Street Opera House, would continue at the new location, but over time, traveling companies would bring all of their own casts, sets and costumes needed for their shows. Ellie Wilton had begun her career in 1871 at the original Piper's, and like her, at least three other thespians went on to join the supporting company of the California Theater. From 1875 to 1878, Ellie Wilton acted at the California Theater. In 1878, she became the leading lady there, where she was accused of being "melodramatic" in her acting style.

Later in the year, the Irish Poets gave literary readings, and the song "The Wearin' of the Green" was used in another production. The theater still respected the audience interest in all things Irish.

Charles Pope became another actor of importance to the new Opera House. He had performed at Maguire's Opera House during the first week of its opening in 1863 and then returned to Virginia City in 1874 and 1878. Born in Germany, Pope began his career in the New York theaters in 1848, coming to California in the mid-1850s and retiring from the stage in the late

This picture of the new Piper's Opera House at the corner of B and Union Streets can be dated to the engagements of Frank Mayo as Davy Crockett, either 1878 or 1882, as the play is advertised on the theater playbill. The front door of the Old Corner Bar is open in this photograph. *History Room, California State Library, Sacramento, CA.*

1880s, having been involved with a number of productions and theaters. Pope built his own theater in St. Louis in 1879. Pope's 1878 return to the new Piper's Opera House found him starring in *Othello* and *Richelieu*. His run was followed by the Kiralfys in the musical ballet fantasy *The Black Crook*.

Barton Hill was stage manager at San Francisco's California Theater in the fall of 1873. Later he bought out a partial ownership of the theater from John McCullough when McCullough returned east in 1877. Born in England, Hill was considered a capable light comedian with extensive East Coast experience. Hill had a long theatrical career, with one highlight being his original direction of Maggie Moore in her signature role in *Struck Oil.* Barton

Actress Ellie Wilton, like many others, worked at the first Piper's Opera House in supporting roles and then progressed to jobs in San Francisco's best theaters. *The Bancroft Library, University of California, Berkeley.*

Hill appeared in advertisements as the acting manager at the new Piper's Opera House in 1879, for shows he brought from California.

Piper created the *Footlight* in the fall of 1872 and, later, possibly *The Daily Stage*, which became advertisement newspapers for his theaters. Realizing the dire financial straits of the theater, in 1879, Lawrence Barrett returned to play at Piper's new theater, reportedly taking no advance money or guarantee of a percentage of money for the engagement, as was usual. Barrett's engagement, the longest run in this theater's history, was recognized as a success and helped the owners at a time when their financial futures were in doubt. Considered one of America's greatest tragedians, Barrett's reputation as an actor of high principle fashioned his legacy as someone who worked hard to improve the state of his art.

Following Barrett were other high-brow performers, including traveling singers the Hyers Sisters and various musicians. Carlotta Patti, a well-known operatic singer, performed in December 1879 in a short engagement with both operatic and popular songs.

On June 23, 1879, an unnamed Virginia City woman wrote to the editor of the *Virginia Evening Chronicle* to offer advice to theater patrons on proper behavior when attending the theater.

> *Sir: I wish you would draw attention to several ill-mannered practices which very much mar the pleasure of attending Piper's Opera House.... The first and most frequent offense against ordinary politeness is the practice a great many men (and I grieve to say some of the gentler sex) have of beating time to the music with their feet or anything else that may be handy, such as a cane or fan. Nothing can be more irritating than this to anyone with nerves. One evening during the engagement of the Hyers Sisters, a man... sat immediately behind me and utterly destroyed my pleasure in the singing*

by thumping away with his cane as if he had been hired to keep time. Such conduct might be pardonable in a gallery boy, but in one who has reached maturity and has ordinary intelligence, it showed a lack of breeding which I think a man ought to hide. On the evening after I had thus been cheated out of an evening's enjoyment…there sat behind me several couples… who behaved in the rudest manner. While the youngest Miss Hyers was singing—and singing beautifully too—these persons whispered and tittered in a way that attracted attention, not only from the distressed audience but from the stage.…It is, of course, impossible to blame Mr. Piper if some who patronize his theater are not capable of behaving themselves like ladies and gentlemen, but there are a few little things he might attend to without disadvantage. A row of legs thrust out over the gallery rail may have its advantages from the picturesque point of view, but it is not altogether a pleasant spectacle. From the dress circle I can see placards on the walls of the gallery forbidding smoking, yet men and boys are permitted always to puff their pipes and cigars. This should not be allowed in any theater in which ladies form a part of the audience.…I wish you would impress upon those who go to the theater that good manners and common sense require that they should do nothing there to disturb those who have paid to see the play and not to endure as calmly as they can the eccentricities of persons whose natural perceptions are dull and whose education has not included the important branch of learning to behave with propriety.
—A Lady Subscriber

It is not known if these comments elicited a change within the typical audience members of Piper's Opera House, but the sentiment of a respectable woman reveals a great deal about issues of class, propriety and expectations within the theater. Moreover, it highlights the new composition of the audience: prominent respectable women.

Women are credited with carrying out a civilizing mission in the West, although they probably didn't think of their lives in those terms. They worked to survive when necessary, understanding the cultural values of respectability and how those values affected them. They were well aware of their losses of respectability by the career choices they made or were forced to fill through necessity. Respectable women made the lives of their family members easier. Husbands provided and protected, values reflected and reinforced by many of the melodramas of the age.

Concepts of the public arena or the public sphere as being available to women in the West take different forms when examining the theater.

PIPER'S OPERA HOUSE

VIRGINIA, NEVADA.

Proprietor and Manager..........JOHN PIPER
Stage Manager......J. H. VINSON | Scenic Artist........W. T. PORTER
Conductor........MR. J. LANGER | Property Master.......C. BOWMAN

PARTICULAR NOTICE.

The Management begs to announce that the entertainment given by the Mme. Renz's Original Female Minstrels, now for the first time visiting this coast, is the only first-class and thoroughly enjoyable Lady Minstrel Combination in the world, and ladies and gentlemen may rest assured that the reputation this company possesses for presenting an entirely novel and chaste performance, would preclude the slightest word or action upon the stage, offensive to a refined audience.

M. B. LEAVITT, Manager.

PROGRAMME!

GRAND OVERTURE..........MME. RENZ'S MINSTRELS
SEE THAT MY GRAVE'S KEPT GREEN..........MISS ROSA LEE
CACKLE, CACKLE..........MR. JAS. ROCHE
KEEP ONE LITTLE KISS FOR ME..........MISS LOUISE MONTAGUE
DARKEY FROM THE SOUTH..........MR. PAUL ALLEN
CHARMGNIE..........MISS ELLA LOVE
MUSICAL FINALE..........MME. RENZ'S MINSTRELS

Three Minutes' Intermission.

M'lle ROSITA LEONIE-The Aerial Queen

MISS LULU MORTIMER--Serio-Comic Balladist

THE LOVE SISTERS

In their Sketch,

Aristocratic Flirtations!

LESTER AND ALLEN

SONG AND DANCE SPECIALTIES.

The famous Duettists, Musical and Character Sketch Artists,

MISS GUSSIE CRAYTON and MR. JAMES MAAS

In their Original Operatic Sketch, written by Jas Maas,

THE CALL BOY?

JACK, Call boy of the Theater } MISS GUSSIE GRAYTON
PRIMA DONNA, }
PAT, Gasman of the Theater..........MR. JAMES MAAS

Concluding with Duet from Lucia De Lammermoor.

This advertisement from *The Daily Stage* dates to March 21, 1878. *Author's collection.*

Herrman the Magician is pictured here on the cover of an early booklet featuring his specialty card tricks. *Author's collection.*

Respectable women could act out in a public sphere their right to request a moralizing influence from theater, as the "lady subscriber" did in her letter. They could and did boycott attractions that did not meet with their idea of respectable entertainment. Respectable women did not choose to socialize with lower-class working women and thus helped enforce the social divisions within society. Respectable women could also enhance education or crusade against challenges to morality within their communities. They could create their own amateur theatrical, musical and literary societies to counter the programming of their local theaters.

Herrman the prestidigitator, the "King of the Wizards," had played the earlier Opera House in 1870 and then returned to Virginia City for one night, December 6, 1879, while on his way to San Francisco. In 1870, he disgorged silver dollars from a man's hat, and his wife sang as part of the entertainment. By 1879, he had progressed to firing a woman out of a cannon. He is an example of one of the many variety performers who trod the boards in Virginia City.

The California Theater experienced a disastrous 1879 as Virginia City's economic depression spread to San Francisco also. Frank Mayo did return to Piper's twice, but these early years of the 1880s drove John Piper to renew some lost moneymaking strategies of the previous decades. He established a roller-skating option at the theater, and progressively, long breaks with short engagements continued throughout the century.

11

PIPER'S OPERA HOUSE LIVES ON

Those who acted under Piper's management in the early days, have left this part of the world, passed away forever. Piper has outlasted two thirds of them and is still hale and hearty, still full of grit and pluck, and expecting to live fifty years longer and build and burn more opera houses.
—Carson City Morning Appeal, *May 8, 1885*

Piper's Opera House, rebuilt at B and Union Streets in 1878, burned to the ground on March 14, 1883. A new theater rebuilt at the same location, opened in 1885 and still stands. Despite lawsuits and challenges to ownership, John kept control of the building and business as his son George became the owner of the rebuilt theater in 1887 through a complicated repurchase. The 1885 theater and saloon were built with reclaimed lumber, resulting in a more utilitarian design. It was never considered as refined as the previous theater on that spot. Forty-five railroad car springs placed under the floor were supposedly an aid to dancers, as the Opera House always needed to provide more than just professional theatricalities. A portrait of William Shakespeare over the proscenium arch heralds the classics, as only four boxes line the walls near the stage. The stage rises four feet from the auditorium floor and originally had gas footlights. Its raked stage—the actors gain elevation as they move away from the audience—is one of only a handful left in the United States. The original chandelier, now electrified, casts a sunburst pattern on the ceiling.

Piper's stock company of actors attached to his earliest theater had been diminished during the five-year lifespan of his second theater and then became nonexistent. John had struggled to get the best actors, whose support of stars could make or break a performance, but those days were ending. The 1880s was a period of transition in the theater business. Combination companies originating in the East or in San Francisco, and touring stars with their own ensembles, ended the need for stock companies attached to every theater. Piper's disbanding of his stock company of supporting actors illuminates a larger picture of the changing times within the American theater business itself.

As the economic depression in Virginia City started in the late 1870s and increased during the 1880s, people moved away. The population declined to only a few thousand by the 1890s, and it was slightly less than 2,700 by 1900. A handful of miners remained on the Comstock, still forming the backbone of the audience members at the theater, which adjusted to present shows with greater appeal to women and children.

The last Piper's Opera House, similar to his earlier ones, enjoyed patriotic celebrations and speeches by local politicians held there on a regular basis. The theater became a place in which politics—discussed, debated and observed—took center stage. Political debates in the theater strengthened the ties of the citizens to the community as a whole. Politics carried out in the theater may have increased this blending of the two forms, politics and entertainment. The increase in lectures during the depression years may have also increasingly met an audience's need for the theater to become a place of intellectual stimulation.

The style of programming that occurred at the two earlier Opera Houses, plays interspersed with variety performers, with occasional lecturers and musical events, continued at the last Piper's Opera House. Other events included prize fighting, sporting contests, social balls, graduations and fraternal organization meetings and events that challenged the theater to become a community center. The Emmett Guard fraternal society used the Opera House annually for a St. Patrick's Day dance. Amateur groups used the Opera House for school plays. Previous historians have searched for stars performing in the historic Piper's Opera House, and a handful did stop on their way to or from San Francisco. But many stars who performed here came toward the end of their careers: Mrs. D.P. Bowers and Harry Courtaine in 1888 and Lydia Thompson, Lotta Crabtree and Frank Mayo in 1889. Younger names would use the Virginia City audiences to hone their skills onstage, as actors had done in the 1860s and 1870s.

This picture of Piper's Opera House, taken in the 1930s, shows the dilapidated state of the building. This is the extant theater, finished in 1885, that is now restored. *Author's collection.*

The Comstock mining boom was effectively over by 1880, and the changes in the theater's ownership and licensing to John Piper's son George reflected legal posturing by the Piper family after they suffered financial setbacks. Miriam Michelson's Comstock history argues that wealthy mine owner John Mackay, a silent partner in the 1885 Opera House operation, became the significant owner. John's nephew Charles Piper substantiated Mackay's financial help to keep the Opera House afloat, which he said was done in return for the permanent use of a box seat by Mackay. Charles recalled that John and Henry huddled together, pen in hand, to calculate the loss of money from the box seat that ultimately proved to be more than they had received from Mackay in support of the Opera House.

Haverly's Minstrels became an institution in Piper's last two Opera Houses, appearing repeatedly. J.H. Haverly created a new genre of minstrelsy that held wide appeal, with more than one troupe performing at a time in the West. They appeared in April 1878 as "refined minstrelsy," later appearing as Haverly's Comedy Company and as Mastodon Minstrels, which were advertised for women and children. In 1879, Haverly's played for five nights as United Mastodon Minstrels. Returning in 1881, 1882, 1885, 1888, 1892, 1895 and 1900, and now called the New

American and European Minstrels, the company increased its number of performers and used extensive scenery. Their engagements in Virginia City were short, lasting only two nights in 1881. With both male and female impersonators, they billed themselves as performing modern, high-class minstrelsy. Haverly based his new minstrelsy on the traditional three-part organization: a musical first part; specialty characterizations from some of the individual members of the troupe, including banjo and jig dancing and a singing female impersonator, in the second part; and then finishing with a comedic one-act play in three scenes. But Haverly sanitized his productions and began using extremely large casts, forty performers in 1878 and one hundred by 1880. They replaced the raucous shows of the 1860s with lavishly produced variety shows suitable for all audiences with a much greater emphasis on popular songs and cheap prices for children. In contrast to the older minstrel style shows, Haverly's Minstrels looked more like revolving vaudeville acts.

This photograph of the theater interior shows the raked stage; one of a handful from the 1800s that remain in the United States. The terms upstage and downstage come from this creation. *Special Collections Photograph, UNRS-P1487-1.tif collection_6081, Special Collections and University Archive Collections, University of Nevada, Reno.*

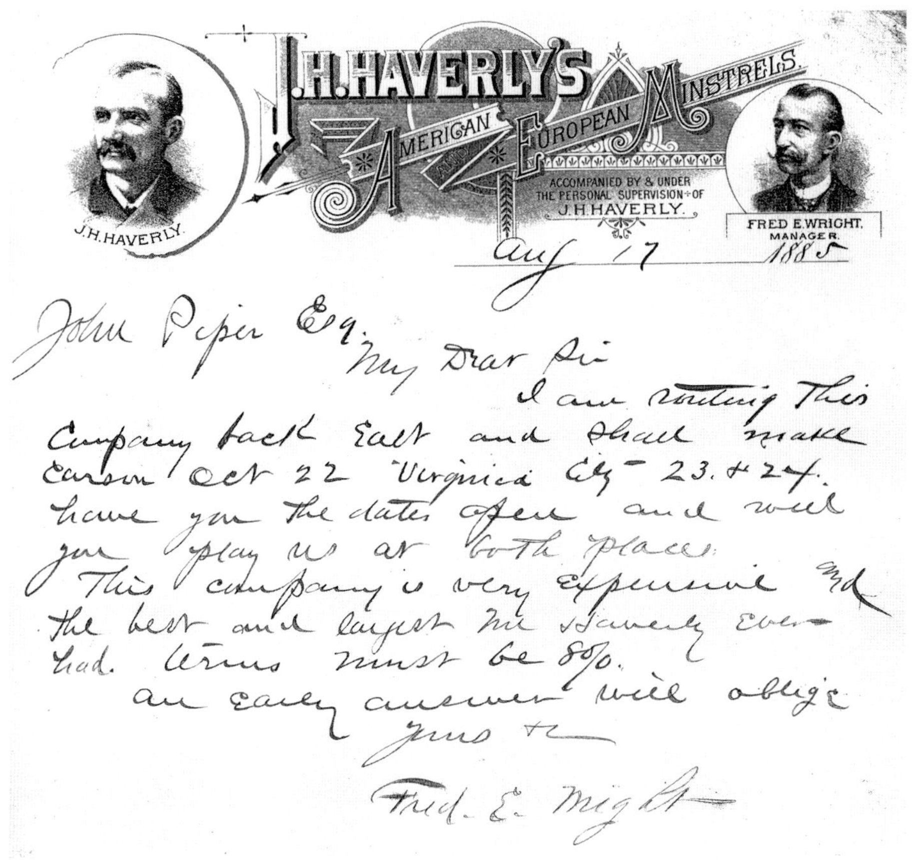

J.H. HAVERLY'S AMERICAN AND EUROPEAN MINSTRELS.
ACCOMPANIED BY & UNDER THE PERSONAL SUPERVISION OF J.H. HAVERLY.
J.H. HAVERLY
FRED E. WRIGHT. MANAGER.

Aug 17 1885

John Piper Esq.
My Dear Sir
I am routing this company back East and shall make Carson Oct 22 Virginia City 23 & 24. have you the dates open and will you play us at both places. This company is very expensive and the best and largest Mr Haverly ever had. terms must be 80%. an early answer will oblige
Yours &c
Fred. E. Wright

The letter between Haverly's Minstrels and John Piper constitutes a performance contract between the two. *John Piper Business Papers, Bancroft Library, University of California, Berkeley; BANC MSS P-G 212, boxes 1–3; box 1, folder 5.*

Haverly's Mastodon Minstrels disbanded in 1896, and J.H. Haverly retired from active management shortly thereafter. He was probably minstrelsy's most successful organizer and promoter, having a good sense of the public's changing tastes and a flair for advertising and producing. When Haverly's minstrels were not available, the Opera House hosted other, lesser-known troupes. On February 1 and 2, 1889, the Georgia minstrels performed with a large cast of Black performers. Beginning in the late 1870s, minstrel casts began employing Black performers, as they could argue that their presentations were more realistic than those of the older-style white actors in blackface makeup. Considered resistance performances, these Black performers sought to redefine Blackness for audiences in much more positive ways that humanized and normalized the assemblage.

The newspapers advertised in February 1885 that the new Opera House would open with a ball and benefit for John Piper, but on March 6, 1885, the theater showed *Peck's Bad Boy.* The play had a short two-night run and then appeared in Carson City before it traveled on to San Francisco's Bush Street Theater. This pattern would become typical. As Virginia City lost its population, John Piper continued his strategy of hosting plays for one or two nights in his hometown and then adding a night each in Carson City and Reno, creating a theatrical circuit in northern Nevada similar to those in other places in the nation. By the 1880s, performers had to be offered nights in neighboring towns to make the trip to Nevada worthwhile.

In July 1885, William Mestayer, a longtime San Francisco actor who had been in the stock company of the California Theater, starred in a short run at Piper's. The six-foot-tall character actor known as a "pantaloon villain," appeared equally comfortable in Shakespearean plays and burlesque performances. Late in 1885, the famous actress Fanny Janauschek, known throughout the world as the queen of tragedy, highlighted the entertainment offerings that year. She had come to the United States in the late 1860s and specialized in Shakespearean roles.

Lillian Smith performed in Piper's Opera House as a champion rifle shot on September 11 and 12, 1885, for three shows. The teenager rivaled Annie Oakley as the best female shootist in the country and became part of *Buffalo Bill's Wild West Show* for roughly three years, as well as others. The newspaper advertisement specifically called women to view the "interesting and instructive" trick shooting as a demonstration of what women could do. "Miss Lillian can shoot and reload 25 times in one minute, and break 25 glass balls," puffed the *Enterprise*.

Other notables who trod the boards that first year included Emma Wixom, known as Emma Nevada, who played in December 1885 for one night. Three hundred people traveled to her concert aboard special trains chartered from Reno and Carson City. The Thompson Opera Company in *The Mikado*, prestidigitators, prize fights and lecturers rounded out the first year.

Lily Langtry performed on July 19, 1887, as she traveled east after touring California. On July 20, she purchased a lot in Carson City and toured Lake Tahoe. Not considered a particularly talented actress, Lily used vehicles that allowed her figure to take center stage. Langtry was known as the Jersey Lily because of her birth on the British island of

Lillian Smith was a crack shot who challenged Annie Oakley's infamy. The two did not get along. *Courtesy of David Baker Jacobs.*

Jersey. She began her acting career in 1881, after scandalous attachments to British royalty. With her first American tour in 1883, she grew in status and became known in the West for her mode of transportation, a private railroad car. December 1887 saw a three-day run with Maude Granger in *The Creole*, *The New Magdalene* and *The Planter's Wife* while she toured with her company. Granger became a national star with a fifty-five-year career that ended in the twentieth century.

Few Nevadans attained national musical success, but Richard "Dickie" Jose, who came to Nevada as a child from Cornwall, England, rose from local acclaim to become celebrated throughout the country. Richard Jose sang at the Opera House in August 1887, accompanied by Flora Finlayson, a contralto. His rich high tenor voice carried sentimental songs in a style that would bring him national prominence as the best ballad singer of the era. Jose, remembered for his signature song "Silver Threads Among the Gold," frequently brought tears to the eyes of the listening public when in performance. His story of singing in Virgina City's saloons was central to his public persona. He sang with a minstrel company in the 1880s and retired when his style became outdated.

Virginia City's Irish community continued to be honored with programming that reflected positive images of Ireland. Late 1888 saw Dan Morris Sullivan's *Mirror of Ireland* with a play entitled *Kitty from Cork*. Three nights over the Fourth of July in 1889 found another Irish play, *The Fairy's Well*, offered.

The Rentz Santley American burlesque company opened for the first time in March 1878 at Piper's second Opera House and returned in 1879 with a show that newspapers felt could have been attended by wives and children. Mabel Santley was the star of the group, which returned to Piper's in 1888, and Ed Piper, John's son, brought them back in 1899. The Rentz Santley Company had been created by M.B. Leavitt based on minstrelsy and older burlesque styles that had been brought to America by British troupes, including Lydia Thompson's. This new style became known as American burlesque, which, by the late 1800s, had begun to be relegated to sleazy dives in large cities, becoming an entertainment form for men only. Mabel Santley's hourglass figure, popular in the 1890s, continued a genre of female shape as an entertainment form in and of itself. Theater managers were criticized for presenting anything available in the way of entertainment by the late 1880s as American burlesque advanced in popularity.

Opposite: Operatic singer Emma Nevada. *Society of California Pioneers.*

Left: Lily Langtry performed for one night at Piper's Opera House in 1887. *Library of Congress.*

Lydia Thompson performed in her last American tour in the late 1880s, which included a stop at Piper's on January 1 and 2, 1889. Advertised as a new English burlesque company, it boasted of fifty people in the cast. Her first trip to Virginia City in 1870 featured a one-week stint for a small but exciting cast performing British burlesque that had developed in London's music halls. Common stories that were known to the audience were burlesqued, with women taking men's roles and the men dressed as women. The novelty of the presentation with cutting parody and comedy made for an exhilarating entertainment genre. Lydia's British burlesque was the origin of the later American burlesque that the Rentz Santley Company perfected. By the time of Lydia's last American tour in 1889, she had modified her British burlesque to be "a big leg show," as observed

Opposite: Mabel Santley was an important component of the Rentz Santley American burlesque company. *Author's collection.*

Right: Lydia Thompson performed at Piper's on her last American tour in 1889. She is pictured here at the height of her career in the late 1870s. *Author's collection.*

by newspaperman Alf Doten. He felt it was not as good as the Rentz Santley Company he had seen a few months before. Lydia disliked the feeling that she was responsible for the rise of American burlesque, which she heartily detested.

Coming to California in 1853, Lotta Crabtree performed throughout the 1850s and 1860s as a child star. As early as 1863, she inspired audiences at Maguire's Virginia City Opera House. She also played Piper's during the boom years. Piper was credited by the *Gold Hill News* as bringing what audiences wanted to see when she opened in *The Little Detective* in 1874. On this trip west, Lotta played only San Francisco's California Theater and then Piper's, indicating some type of agreement with John McCullough and Piper for her stop in the mining town. In her 1874 run, Lotta offered *Zip, or Point Lynde Light*, complete with songs and dances that packed in one of the largest audiences ever witnessed. Special trains were chartered to bring Carson City folks to the shows, and John Piper personally escorted Lotta through a tour of the mines.

Lotta charmed audiences with breakdowns, clog dances and banjo solos. With sensational, sentimental melodramas written especially for her, such as *The Little Detective*, Lotta played several roles to showcase her humor, impersonations and musical talents. In later years, Lotta would recall having played *The Little Detective* "season after season and year after year, until I am really ashamed to show my face in it upon the stage again." She paid a quarter for the play that made her "thousands upon thousands."

Lotta Crabtree, pictured here as a young performer. Frequently copied, Lotta has become an icon of nineteenth-century Western theater history. *Author's collection.*

Lotta dominated all other female performers from 1865 to 1885, a spectacular career. Often mimicked by others, Lotta returned to Virginia City in 1889 on her last national tour. At well over forty years old, Lotta mugged and cavorted for miners with their pants stuffed in their boot tops. The protean star giggled, twirled her finger in her dimple and flashed her stockinged legs in innocent joyousness; mischievous flirtations that recalled her best years as a child star. The play's plot was extraneous. Author and actress Helen Bates toured with Lotta at that time and noted bearded miners threw coins on stage for her. Picking up every coin, Lotta stashed them away in her bodice and stockings, giving audience members a glimpse at her legs. Lotta played the banjo for them, whirled the banjo, laughed and joked, her only banjo performance on this last tour. Because of Lotta's formidable and overprotective mother, she retired as one of the wealthiest performers of her generation, a versatile performer to whom other actresses were frequently compared.

Harry Courtaine returned to America in 1888 for a few years, touring to Virginia City for one night in *Little Puck*. He did enjoy a successful year in New York, which ended when he fell off the wagon and requested that a judge place him in jail to sober up—the same ploy used by Tom Maguire in early San Francisco. The New York judge requested social services interventions for the comic actor. Dublin-born Courtaine died in Manhattan in 1910.

Emma Hanley appeared in the supporting cast of *Little Puck* with Harry Courtaine. Her best career years were 1884 to 1890. *Author's collection.*

Frank Mayo in a coonskin cap as Davy Crockett at the height of his career. *History Room, California State Library, Sacramento, CA.*

Frank Mayo returned to Virginia City on November 7, 1889, for one last night of *Davy Crockett*, a play he had presented to the townsfolk in 1874, 1878 and 1882. Then, by traveling the country, he had presented Davy to thousands of people. Actors were subject to role entrapment throughout the nineteenth century. Their performances of a specific role led to ever-increasing interest by patrons. The sayings "Davy, bar the door," and "Be sure you're right, then go ahead," passed into popular usage because of this play. Returning to northern Nevada in 1889, Mayo was toward the end of a spectacular career. Of the twenty-odd years that he played the role of Davy, he became interchangeable with the character in the minds of his spectators. Mayo believed that versatility anchored a stock actor's success, but the public wanted an "identity" in a star. In later years, Mayo executed the title role in *Puddin'head Wilson*, based on Mark Twain's novel. He became one of the country's most successful, best-known and beloved actors. He performed up to the day before his death in 1896.

Other lesser performers finished out the year 1889; some were not national stars, but they were practiced on Western stages. Isabel Morris appeared in October for an engagement that included *Hazel Kirke* in Carson City and *East Lynne* at Piper's Opera House. Morris, known for her expressive face, performed in California during the 1880s and had just returned from a tour of Australia, where she had used *Lady of Lyons*—a play then over fifty years old—as a featured vehicle. She was followed by Margaret Mather in *Romeo and Juliet*, her signature play that garnered many encomiums for her interpretation. Mather enjoyed a short sixteen-year career, which started in Chicago in 1882.

A winter storm in 1890 overloaded the roof of the Opera House, which collapsed onto the theater level and required substantial rebuilding before shows could continue. The 1891 events of the season included *Shenandoah* and appearances by Joseph Grismer and Phoebe Davies in *Beacon Lights* and

Lights and Shadows for a two-night run. Other noteworthy performers who stopped at Piper's Opera House included Jennie Yeamans. Born in Australia in 1862 to a theatrical family, Jennie became a child star in the 1870s and 1880s, performing in Nevada in September 1893. She enjoyed a successful run of three hundred nights in New York. She later participated in a benefit performance for survivors of the San Francisco earthquake.

Attendance to shows in the early 1890s dropped in price to less than a dollar per seat, as the Panic of 1893 swept the country. In 1894, the theater's orchestra leader offered a "Grand Social and dance school," charging men fifty cents and allowing women free entrance. In 1896, singers Sam Shaw and Jessie Shirley continued with ticket prices set at ten, twenty and thirty cents a person for their shows. By 1898, the prices had increased to fifty and seventy-five cents for admission to a musical satire of the play *Wild Oats*.

Starring actresses appeared for one night only as the depression deepened. Other strategies included unusual entertainment, like mock boxing contests offered by prizefighter James Corbett. February 1897 brought a rare play, *Si Perkins*, a Yankee-character comedy featuring Sam J. Burton and Lillie Coleman. The show received a very positive review in the *Territorial Enterprise*. John Phillip Sousa's fifty-piece orchestra appeared for one night on March 4, 1896, in one of the more famous showings at the Opera House. Later in 1896, Zamloch the magician appeared but used an old gimmick to attract audiences. He gave gifts and small presents to the audience members, a depression strategy that had been used at least thirty years previously. The *Territorial Enterprise* considered him mystifying, equal to Herrman or Kellar, magicians who had performed in years past.

The economic depression during the 1890s brought back some questionable programming. Probably targeted at men only, Duncan Clark's female minstrels appeared on August 30, 1892. And, in 1895, a "London Gaity Girl" with "Pretty English Beauties" performed for one night. The show starred Marion Nolan, who was remembered as the original California Venus. The year 1896 saw Miss Gracie Plaisted with her musical comedy company. Lecturers stopped at the theater, and many nights of balls, social meetings with dances, political debates and political lectures during the 1890s reflected the rise of the Silver Party in Nevada.

Although it was generally known as a forum for melodrama and classic plays, Virginia City's theaters, in reality, offered more nights of variety entertainment than legitimate theater. Variety theatricalities included minstrelsy, the most popular of the variety styles, while musicians, magicians, tight rope walkers, child prodigies, animal acts, gymnasts, contortionists, ventriloquists, panoramas, strong men and women, lecturers and anyone with a promotional gimmick filled theaters with performers who were willing and able to travel to the mining town.

Theater spoke to the audience's needs. Theatricalities with special appeal to the Irish, who enjoyed the largest population numbers, included plays and minstrel shows with common Irish ballads, Irish performers and nostalgic scenes of home. As the population aged, second-generation Irish immigrants loved Dion Boucicault's plays that defined Irish identity for younger people who had no memory of their parents' homeland. The later 1800s saw a change from the Irish immigrant to the Irish American. Theater production changed to include the three-wall box set, while light opera, greater realism and "cup and saucer" dramas became popular.

Does the tradition of the extant Piper's Opera House hosting the best players in America hold up to detailed investigation? Not completely. The best years of 1874 and 1875 occurred in the D Street theater, which is long gone. Many good players appeared at the current Piper's Opera House, built in 1885, but many noteworthy players of the age did not. The determining factor for the attraction of an actor to play Piper's was their work in San Francisco. Many East Coast actors never toured the West, and many who did tour the West did not play Piper's. As time progressed during the late 1800s, many of the performers at Piper's extant Opera House performed in California theaters and were not well known nationally. Performers with significant national careers, like Lotta Crabtree, appeared there toward the end of their lives. Additionally, one-night engagements were common, as presumably all interested townspeople could attend on one night in a theater that today holds roughly four hundred people.

John Piper passed away in 1897, but even previous to his death, his son Edward had taken over some of his management duties. In the early 1900s, the theater was used as a silent movie house, perhaps playing movies with some of its previous stars in crossover roles in cinema. The theater remained closed for much of the twentieth century until it was reopened as a museum in the 1940s. Now under restoration with federal and state monies, it is run as an events center through the Virginia City Tourism Commission.

BIBLIOGRAPHY

Bates, Helen Marie. *Lotta's Last Season.* Private printing by Hildreth and Company, 1940.

Belasco, David. "My Life's Story." *Hearst's Magazine,* June 1914. 767–779.

Clark, Susie C. *John McCullough as Man, Actor, and Spirit.* Broadway Publishing Company, 1914.

Crane, William H. *Footprints and Echoes.* E.P. Dutton and Company, 1927.

DeAngelis, Jefferson, and Alvin Harlow. *A Vagabond Trouper.* Harcourt, Brace and Company, 1931.

Eichin, Carolyn Grattan. "From Sam Clemens to Mark Twain: Sanitizing the Western Experience." *The Mark Twain Annual* 12 (2014): 113–35.

———. *From San Francisco Eastward, Victorian Theater in the American West.* University of Nevada Press, 2020.

———. "The Piper Brothers' Business of Amusements: Piper's Corner Bar." *Nevada Historical Society Quarterly* 56, nos. 3–4 (Fall/Winter 2013): 151–66.

Farquhar, Francis, ed. *Up and Down California in 1860–1864; The Journal of William H. Brewer.* University of California Press, 2003.

Hutton, Lawrence. *Curiosities of the American Stage.* Harper and Brothers, 1891.

Jennings, John J. *Theatrical and Circus Life, or Secrets of the Stage, Green Room, and Stardust Arena.* St. Louis Historical Publishing, 1882.

Leathes, Edmund. *An Actor Abroad.* Hurst and Blackett, 1880.

Leavitt, M.B. *Fifty Years in Theatrical Management.* Broadway Publishing Company, 1912.

Leman, Walter. *Memories of an Old Actor.* A. Roman Comp., 1886.

McGrath, Roger. *Gunfighters, Highwaymen and Vigilantes, Violence on the Frontier.* University of California Press, 1984.

Michelson, Miriam. *The Wonderlode of Silver and Gold*. The Stratford Company, 1935.

Miller, William Charles. "An Historical Study of Theatrical Entertainment in Virginia City, Nevada or Bonanza and Borasca Theatres on the Comstock." 2 vols. PhD diss., University of Southern California, 1947.

Morris, Clara. *Life on the Stage, My Personal Experiences and Recollections.* McClure, Phillips, 1901.

Odell, George C.D. *Annals of the New York Stage*. 17 vols. Columbia University Press, 1945.

Piper, John. Bankruptcy Case Number 3325, U.S. District Court, NV, 1879. Record Group 21 U.S. District Court, District of Nevada, Bankruptcy Case Files, Act of 1875–78, boxes 1–15. Federal Archives and Records Center, San Bruno, CA.

———. Business Papers 1877–1918. BANC MSS P-G 212, boxes 1–3. Bancroft Library, University of California, Berkeley.

Powell, John J. *The Land of Silver*. Bacon, 1876.

Scharnhorst, Gary. *The Life of Mark Twain, the Early Years*. University of Missouri Press, 2018.

Taylor, Joe H. *Joe H. Taylor Barnstormer; His Travels, Troubles, and Triumphs During Fifty Years in Footlight Flashes*. William Jenkins Company, 1913.

Van Tilburg Clark, Walter. *The Journals of Alfred Doten, 1849–1903*. Vols. 1–3. University of Nevada Press, 1973.

Watson, Margaret G. *Silver Theatre; Amusements of Nevada's Mining Frontier 1850–1864*. Arthur Clark Company, 1964.

Whiffen, Mrs. Thomas (Blanche Galton). *Keeping Off the Shelf*. E.P. Dutton and Co., 1928.

Newspapers include:

Boston Herald
Carson City Appeal
Daily Alta California (San Francisco)
Daily Trespass (Virginia City)
Eureka (Nevada)Daily Sentinel
Gold Hill (Nevada) News
Nevada State Journal (Reno)
New York Dramatic Mirror
New York Herald
Reno Gazette

Sacramento Daily Record-Union
Sacramento Daily Union
San Francisco Call
San Francisco Dramatic Chronicle
San Jose Herald
Stockton Daily Herald
Territorial Enterprise (Virginia City, Nevada)
Virginia Evening Chronicle (Virginia City, Nevada)